"The root texts of Buddhism and Zen from India, China, Korea, and Japan offer many expressions of their ground as earth wisdom. Zenju Earthlyn Manuel's experiences of indigenous African, Caribbean, and Native American shamanic practice illuminate her descriptions of the inner value of Zen ceremonies, spaces, and invoking of spiritual ancestors. This valuable book includes helpful guidance, such as her discussion of the shamanic quality of Zen chanting. Zenju speaks in deeply personal rather than theoretical terms about the underlying shamanic reality of Zen practice. Such awareness is crucial for the development of contemporary Western Zen."
—Taigen Dan Leighton, author of *Just This Is It*

"This book will turn your conception of Zen inside out. Following on scholarly work on Buddhist Modernism (the Western attempt to 'clean up' Buddhism for a secular scientific audience), *The Shamanic Bones of Zen* pulls us back us to the sacred depth of BuddhaDharma, reclaiming Buddhism's original, and, perhaps, subversive spirit of connection to earth, mystery, and soul. Informed by the diverse and intensely intuitive spiritual practice she engaged in before she came to Zen, Zenju Earthlyn Manuel's thorough reframing of the tradition is eye-opening, poetic, and inspiring. The book ends with her original liturgical poems, texts I hope will be chanted in Zen centers someday."
—Norman Fischer, author of *When You Greet Me I Bow*

"This generous book gifts us with a voice divine and divining. Zenju's reverence for ritual beckons us home: into a rootedness deeper than the earth, a vastness bigger than the sky."
—Chenxing Han, author of *Be the Refuge: Raising the Voices of Asian American Buddhists*

"The shamanic bones of Zen are buried in plain sight. But sometimes we need a masterful practitioner and writer like Zenju Earthlyn Manuel to shine a light and open our eyes. I bow to her in gratitude."
—Hozan Alan Senauke, author of *The Bodhisattva's Embrace: Dispatches from Engaged Buddhism's Front Lines*

THE
SHAMANIC
BONES *of*
ZEN

Revealing the Ancestral Spirit and
Mystical Heart of a Sacred Tradition

Zenju Earthlyn Manuel

FOREWORD BY
Dr. Paula Arai

SHAMBHALA

Shambhala Publications, Inc.
2129 13th Street
Boulder, Colorado 80302
www.shambhala.com

Cover art: Carole Hénaff
Cover design: Kate E. White
Interior design: Lora Zorian

9 8 7 6 5 4 3 2

Printed in the United States of America

Shambhala Publications makes every effort to print on acid-free,
recycled paper.

Shambhala Publications is distributed worldwide by
Penguin Random House, Inc., and its subsidiaries.

Library of Congress Cataloging-in-Publication Data

Names: Manuel, Zenju Earthlyn, author. |
Arai, Paula Kane Robinson, writer of foreword.
Title: The shamanic bones of Zen: revealing the ancestral spirit and
mystical heart of a sacred tradition / Zenju Earthlyn Manuel;
foreword by Paula Arai.
Description: Boulder: Shambhala, 2022.
Identifiers: LCCN 2021039380 | ISBN 9781611809190 (trade paperback)
Subjects: LCSH: Zen Buddhism—Rituals. | Buddhism—Rituals. |
Zen Buddhism. | Buddhism.
Classification: LCC BQ9270.2.M36 2022 | DDC 294.3/43—dc23
LC record available at https://lccn.loc.gov/2021039380

The soft breath of the ancestors touched my face with the sun this morning. I awakened in the sweetness left on my skin last night—the scent of pine and cedar from wood burned in the fire. And the pain is not the problem. It is evidence of life that is older than redwood trees.

Contents

Foreword

While reading *The Shamanic Bones of Zen*, I saw a documentary on elephants navigating ancient routes across the African continent in their annual migration between habitats with sufficient water. Passing through harsh environments, they arrived at a watering hole that had dried up. Before despair set in, a mother elephant gently picked up a bone of an elephant who had not survived a past journey. She tenderly passed it to her calf to hold. This poignantly deliberate act conveyed the gravity of respecting forebears, humility in the face of nature's cycles, and gratitude for the support of others. Safe passage depends on ritualized actions that intimately connect ancestors and living beings, imparting wisdom that transcends birth and death. In this sense, elephants are shamanic beings.

Attuning to the dynamic activity of being-time, Zenju Oshō unearths the bones of Zen. She discerns that these venerable bones consist of immeasurable forces not subject to ordinary cause and effect or fully controllable by human effort, and she feels the pulse of shamanic sensibilities coursing through Zen practices and teachings. The author illuminates how Zen practice offers numerous portals to the flow of intimate interconnections wherein liberating transformation occurs. Communing and communicating with beings one has never met is shamanic activity. Making offerings to ancestors and those whom one does not know or love personally is shamanic activity. To bow in gratitude to those who have caused harm is shamanic activity. Zazen is a ritualized act that opens one's heart to grow, expand, and connect, enabling one to hear crying, even when sitting quietly alone. Attuning to the rhythms of earth, air, water, and fire and offering one's whole self for awakening—for compassion to all—is shamanic activity. When steeped in a shamanic modality that dissolves limitations and expands awareness, Zen practices and teachings galvanize boundless embodied activity and amplify transformative power. Shamanic Zen thrives in conditions that are imponderable, painful, and elusive. Practicing in a shamanic mode heals wounds generated by delusion, greed, hatred, and oppression. Like glaciers, most of its massive activity occurs below the surface.

Perhaps the shamanic dimension of Zen has receded into the shadows because in America Zen is characterized as a tradition that cultivates the kind of thinking associated with a scientific perspective. A shamanic perspective is not incompatible with modern science, but those who prefer clear reasoning and being in control often downplay or ignore this central aspect of Zen. To speak openly about this dimension of Zen displays Zenju's courage, her courageous love.

The shamanic bones of Zen are porous. They have not been molded to reinforce sectarian authority or official institutional structures. The bones are infused with vibrant streams of indigenous traditions that transform teachings and practices in order to provide native nutrients for thriving in local conditions. In accordance with the vow to liberate all beings, any barriers that stand in the way of compassion must be dismantled, and anything that serves compassion can be enlisted. Zenju Oshō acknowledges these creative currents as she transmutes available resources to shed light on suffering.

Zenju Oshō teaches how a shamanic mode of Zen offers a way to awaken to peace while remaining attuned to the painful reality that we all suffer when people angrily harm others, deliberately leverage power to serve the select few, or ignore the insidious systems that undergird injustice. As humans we are organic, impermanent forms of congealed earth who channel water, animate fire, and circulate air, and we are capable of embodying flowing wellsprings of love. With piercing clarity, Zenju challenges her readers with a pointed question, "Are you willing to experience love?"

To read this book is to enter a sanctuary that inspires openness and growth. Guiding us to breathe ourselves back to immeasurable love, Zenju Oshō empowers and affirms each person in their particular embodied form. She invites us on a path that leads to the boundless flux of a liberating home, a home fortified with tender and fierce acts of compassion, a home where people crying "I can't breathe!" are heard, a home that generates safe conditions for all to be at peace. This is the marrow of the shamanic bones of Zen.

—PAULA ARAI

Rattling the Bones

I enter the zendo without a sound. I sit in my designated chair. The cold of winter causes me to wrap my light wool robe tighter around my body. The bells are ringing and drums are playing. I bow when the head teacher passes. I smell the earth, mold instead of incense. The seeing begins when all is quiet and still. But my breath is not there. I can't breathe. I can no longer sit up. My body leans. Am I dying? Fear rises. I had not been feeling well. I don't look around. I am only with this dying, my heart out of rhythm. I hear the words, "You are going to be fine." I feel myself being shepherded into death by those talking to me. I flinch and then notice a sudden joy that someone is speaking to me while I am dying. That there will be someone or something there to lovingly lead me to my death.

Once, a seer said to me, "You know they aren't doing nothing but magic over there where you are." I asked, "Where? Who?" She said, "Those people running around in black. They're doing witchcraft and it's dangerous the way they are doing it." She was talking about the Zen center where I was training. I laughed but heeded the warning in my own way. I didn't leave. I was already one of those witches, so to speak.

I was drawn to Soto Zen Buddhist practice (Soto is one of many Zen traditions) because of the ancient rituals, ceremonies, and silence. It felt familiar: the incense burning, the bowing, the quiet, the chanting, the black, the firelit candles, a feeling of floating in darkness. Obviously, I found the experience of Zen very different from the institutions that offer an environment to practice Zen. I found a Zen of the earth, deep in the muck of human conditions including racism, sexism, and homophobia.

Zen has not been my only practice community, and it was not my first within Buddhism. While practicing Nichiren Buddhism, I found the gateway of Buddhism amid xenophobia. And, in spiritual communities of color, I witnessed experiences of internalized oppression wreaking havoc among their members. Fortunately, all of what the world brings into the gateway furthers the significance of our spiritual prayers and meditations. There is no religious tradition, institution, or spiritual community in the United States that is without systemic oppression. It is the soil by which we are given to dig out liberation every moment, in an endless garden.

There are many roads by which one can access the freedom taught by sages, prophets, and medicine people. I chose Zen as one of a few roads in my life. It became my activism after organizing communities for most of my young adult life. Nowhere else than Zen could I find an environment or practice where I could make *daily* ritual offerings in community, including my very breath, for the sake of humanity.

Many people see ritual as a means by which organized religions govern the behavior of their adherents. Robert Scharf, a scholar and professor of Buddhist studies, writes, "Some scholars have argued that [Buddhist] ritual . . . legitimizes local norms and values by casting them as an integral part of the natural order of things." In other words, ritual, because it is steeped in authority (who is authorized and who isn't), can have a conservative and coercive nature that remains concealed from view. Although there can be deception and false consciousness in ritual, I hold that the ritual remains in the practice of it. "Participation in a living ritual tradition reaches beyond the vagaries of the intellect to one's somatic being," writes Scharf, describing this alternative view.[1]

Can we experience transformation through ritual, alone in our own homes? Maybe yes, maybe no. In Zen, ritual is done in ceremony with others. For me, following ancient rituals of traditional paths is to walk an age-old path proven to assist people in transforming suffering into awakening. Rituals—done on a daily basis, or as part of ceremony—create an atmosphere of touching the bones: something entirely different than rituals used for social order or coercion.

. °.

My bones were rattled. I was shaken by the visions that came during chanting, zazen (sitting meditation), rituals, and ceremonies. The visions loosened the tight hinges, exposing the chaos of the world while revealing a layer of life behind our physical existence.

There is an invisible experience rarely talked about in Zen communities. I experienced Zen practice as a shamanic journey of the spirit, and I have found this to be true for many other practitioners. I have written about suffering, particularly as a person affected by systems of oppression in my country. I found ritual and ceremony in my life to be the most profound way to enter into a realm of liberation and embody compassion for my life and all others.

I have participated in many rituals and ceremonies,

including those from African and Native American cultures. Yet it was the Buddhist rituals, practiced on a *daily* basis, that became for me a constant visceral enactment of honoring ancestors while hatred swirled around my head. It was touching the earth in the bow. Honoring the earth as ancestor by putting my head down to receive its blessing. Would I ever accomplish the profound presence of the great sages or shamans of Buddhism? This was not the point. With the smell of burning incense, I could stand next to an agarwood tree ten thousand miles away. The candlelight in the dark zendo was the fire by which life on earth came into being. The darkness was a place to be born in or die in. Whether others in Zen practice had this experience or even talked about their Zen practice in such a way was a moot point. There was a definite experience in Zen and Buddhism of deepening my relationship with the unseen, with spirit worlds and altered states of consciousness.

One might wonder how so much can arise from the simple practices of sitting, chanting, bowing. But even such a bare practice did not spring up from shallow ground without roots and bones. There is nothing pure in a world of interrelationship and history. It is said that even the ancestors are in the womb of Mother Earth, still giving birth. We are them.

. ° .

Here's the disclaimer before we go on: Soto Zen is not considered a shamanic practice by many, and it is not generally taught as one. But if you consider the indigenous beginnings of all cultures, it becomes clear there are underlying esoteric, mystical, or shamanic histories to all spiritualities and religions. Writings about shamanic Buddhism have mostly centered on traditions in Mongolia, Shinto and Shingon in Japan, and Tibetan Buddhism. I am choosing to explore shamanism within Zen to fill in a missing consideration of that tradition. And I am doing so primarily from an experiential point of view, specifically, because most of the writings on shamanic elements of Buddhism are of a scholarly nature and little has been published about experiencing the enchantment of Zen practice. Rarely do you hear of Zen, and especially Soto Zen, in the discourse of shamanism.

Yet, as Sam van Schaik writes in his book *Tibetan Zen*, there existed an ancient Tibetan version of the tradition, originally brought to Tibet by Chinese scholars and monks in the eighth century.[2] Although Tibetan Zen was eventually censored due to doctrinal contradictions between pre-existing Buddhist traditions in the region, the Tibetans seriously considered it as a practice—and practiced it for centuries—in part because Zen at the time contained shamanic practices of divination, spells for various occasions, and the making of amulets and talismans. During its time in Tibet, Zen also incorporated elements of the shamanic Tantric Buddhism. Some of the bones of those ancient practices survived and are included, whether we know it or not, in our practice of Zen today.

To say Zen is "shamanic" can conjure all sorts of fears of magic and the unseen. This concern has a long history, one that has been recast in modern terms. Buddhist studies scholar T. Griffith Foulk, in his essay "Denial of Ritual in the Zen Buddhist Tradition," describes a vision of Zen put forward by Japanese and Western scholars and practitioners since the late nineteenth century.[3] Relying on heavily decontextualized

Song dynasty writings, this particular representation of Zen shows it as a pure form of Buddhist practice without merit, spirits, ghosts, rituals, or magical chanting spells. Far from including shamanic ritual, this view of Zen questions all the school's traditional forms including, at times, meditation.

Zen has been condemned for being over ritualistic, and, in some cases, its ritual side has been laughed at. Perhaps because it is understood that many of the rituals in Buddhist traditions predate Buddhism, they are not taken seriously. Yet Zen Buddhism, even in modern times, has not somehow escaped from the shamanic ritualism of the lands where it was incubated. Therefore, its bones can be found in non-Buddhist traditions like Confucianism and Taoism as well as other Buddhist schools such as Tiantai, Huayen, Vajrayana, Pure Land, Shinto, and Shingon. Even if one looks to Zen's influences from early Buddhist traditions, the story is the same. In Burmese Theravada Buddhism, for instance, there are accounts of how many lay Buddhists in Myanmar form affective relations with wizards in dreams, visions, and through wizards' material embodiments of power. These wizards or shamans serve as bestowers of good luck, defenders of the faith, and spirit guides.

The anti-ritual voice among Zen practitioners in the modern era is not without precedent. The claims made by prominent twentieth-century Zen writers, such as D. T. Suzuki, that the essence of Zen is *satori* (sudden awakening experiences) rather than any form of ritual practice were based on interpretations of teachings from ancient Chinese masters. There are many writings by early Zen masters, such as the renowned Huangbo, that seem to debunk forms, rituals, and ceremony as distractions, as seeking or striving for something out of the ordinary. As Foulk has written though, such writings, seen in their cultural and historical context, were meant to be rhetorical and political rather than literal. He writes: "As I see it, both the idea of ritual as an identifiable type of human behavior, and the tendency to denigrate ritual activity as something that is grounded in irrational or superstitious beliefs, are products of the age of enlightenment in the West and the efforts of European intellectuals to come to grips with foreign cultures they encountered in the course of world exploration and colonial expansion."[4]

I think Foulk is right that there is a modern and Western twist to the anti-ritual voice. Yet I also know that the domination and oppression of the less powerful have been going on for ages, in Asia as well as the West. So I am led to wonder: Is the anti-ritual voice in Zen, justified by the teachings on emptiness, a denouncement of indigenous peoples and shamanic ways of being? If there was rejection of ritual in medieval China, was that an attempt to "clean" Zen of its shamanic roots?

Zen master Lin Chi (Rinzai) said, "From the beginning there is nothing to do."[5] I hold that we are *doing nothing* of our ordinary lives while enacting the forms of Zen. That in fact the forms and rituals are meant to encourage non-doing, in a state of no-mind or no-thought. And, in their mundane redundancy, the rituals teach us how to embody contemplative action when *doing* is necessary.

In fact, the forms reveal that there is nothing to practice. We are *being* in the form. One cannot think of a to-do list while bowing. In the bowing, using the body, there is a chance to experience wellness and transformation, even though the goal is to achieve nothing—similar to how others pray and the results of those prayers are unknown. The nothingness, for me, was the environment in which I experienced peace and was able to access wisdom previously unavailable. The trouble comes when the prayers or the forms have no significance and the doing becomes habitual or gets trapped in controlling the practice. The trouble comes when those who are not aware of the spirit of the forms use them without understanding or to show achievement. It comes when the forms are used to establish authority or to sustain a hierarchy rather than as a portal to depth, insight, and wisdom for the sake of humanity.

⁰ ⁰ ⁰

These are my questions: Are we practicing in a tradition, Buddhism, that was at times enforced by rulers who dominated over the people of the farms and rural areas in Asia? Did indigenous peoples of South Asia, Central Asia, and East Asia sustain their rituals as an act of resistance? Was this a way of coping with Buddhist traditions adopted at the state level and foreign to their cultures, not unlike when enslaved Africans brought their rituals, deities, and ceremonies into the Christianity that was forced upon them? Is this the source of the remnants we so fortunately have of ancient ways of healing and transformation?

⁰ ⁰ ⁰

By participating in Zen rituals and ceremonies, there was a strong sense in me that something had been suppressed in the transmission of the practice. This strong sense brought me even closer to the practice. I wondered: if the shamanic bones or the indigenous roots that were suppressed in the rising of Buddhism were unearthed, would the practice make more sense to practitioners, especially to black, indigenous, and people of color? What also might be familiar to black, indigenous, and people of color is how, when an indigenous religion is suppressed, aspects of their practices are brought into the religion that is being used to attempt to dominate the people. In premodern Japan, the indigenous religion was the shamanic practice of Shinto. Shinto and many other indigenous practices of China, Japan, Korea, and other countries were sometimes suppressed when the emperors and the people of the land took on the Buddhist practice from India.

It's a complicated history. Sometimes state sponsorship of Buddhism would be reversed; Buddhist monastics and institutions would come under attack from nativist intellectuals and new regimes, as what happened in Japan in the late nineteenth century. Yet my questions remain: When we turn away from rituals and ceremonies in Zen or Buddhism, are we turning away from what little is left that the indigenous people contributed to the practice or used to sustain themselves in the practice? Are we turning away from the sacred embedded in the tradition, even if the idea of sacredness has not been planted deeply into the Western translation of Buddhism? What might we gain from being open to indigenous or shamanic interpretations of Buddhist practice?

I often felt my ancestors at ease with my practice of Zen. I felt they had led me through other traditions to this practice of ritual and ceremony. I had participated in rituals and ceremonies of African and Native American traditions but was not trained completely in them. I had not been fused into priesthood in the African tradition with my Orisha (spirit) over my head. Even though I was a drum and song leader in the Native American Sundance tradition, I was not a sundancer or pipe carrier.

During my long history with the black church, I saw that subtle shades of African culture existed there. Yet my church, as black as it was, had neither musical instruments nor any swaying, clapping, or dancing. However, our a cappella singing in four-part harmony brought "soul" to our church. The Church of Christ, often mistaken for the Church of God in Christ (more commonly known as COGIC), grew out of the Restoration Movement of the early nineteenth century. Led by Thomas Campbell in Cane Ridge, Kentucky, the Restoration Movement had a focus on communion, repentance, baptism, and a cappella singing of hymns—a kind of Christian primitivism or apostolic meant to get the congregation as close as possible to the word of the Bible in the times it was written. Almost anything with an African flavor was suppressed. Since there were no missionaries in this kind of Christianity, it is unclear how black people created their own Churches of Christ. In my own family, my mother was once Baptist but moved toward the conservative style of the Church of Christ, possibly as a way of appearing less poor, southern, and uneducated.

The influence of this "bare" kind of Christianity was instilled in me at a young age. I am sure it contributed to my ease with Buddhism, in particular Japanese Buddhism, where simplicity is at the heart of the practice. I left the church, my first tribe, for many reasons, including the denial of women to preach. I was clear that teaching was on my horizon, and I would not be trained to do such at my conservative black church. The place where my ancestors reached me was in the practice of Nichiren Buddhism and Zen, where I was led to just be. The ancestors needed me to be still and breathe as they approached with what they had to offer my life. It would be these ancestors who guided my Buddhist walk. Buddhism was a path where I found myself communing with ancestors and being guided by them every day, and not only in occasional ceremony.

Many have asked the reason I was drawn to Zen. I was asked this question by people from different races, and I imagine some made the inquiry because of my black skin. Many tried to answer this question for me by saying, "Suffering." Yes, there was suffering. Some have said, "Perhaps you wanted to escape the world." Yes, to listen to what the earth has to say. To gather the medicine, I had to leave the chaos of the world. It is good to escape that which binds you.

When I reflect on the question here, I look back and see myself dressed in clothes meant to enhance the sitting practice (robes and loose Japanese-style pants and tops). I sensed relief from the world without the clothes of the world. My shaved head felt natural. I felt a part of the many African women I have seen, who keep their heads shaved. Walking without shoes had been my favorite thing to do since childhood, so walking in the temple without shoes felt natural. As a child, I was an early sitter. I liked to sit or swing in the backyard, doing what my mother called "daydreaming." She was constantly calling me back to earth.

The Zen poetry of joy and sorrow was like my own poetry that I had been writing since the age of eight, trying to sort out life as a black girl child. In essence, Zen practice immediately felt like me. It was not Zen practice as it was (and is) being talked about by Zen teachers or written about in books. It was not the dogma, the promises of ordination, or the rules of Zen community that drew me in. Despite the practitioners of Western Zen Buddhism being overwhelmingly white and predominantly male at the time of my entrance into the gateway, I experienced an unexplainable peace and transformation with the rituals and ceremonies. These helped me navigate the oppression within the Zen center, which was very much like that within the world at large. Through ritual and ceremony, I was able to transform my internalized oppression into enchantment, accessible within.

When I would walk about under the influence of the atmosphere of stillness and the teachings, I sensed an ancient time that could have been on any continent on the planet, silently witnessing life through connections with people and the land. There was a memory in my bones of something old. I saw myself sharing those teachings.

When I first entered the zendo at Tassajara Zen Center in the Los Padres Forest, I said to myself, "I've been here before." It wasn't the center as much as it was the feeling of being next to the mountains and spending time under the stars at night. Coming to chant and bow, I knew this life, this living close to the earth. I felt myself on the way back, as I walked the old dirt roads in the forest. I felt quite separate at times from the others for some obvious reasons, but also for reasons not so obvious. The separation served me. I was constantly having a shamanic experience of the land, the rituals, and the ceremonies coming up through my bones. Zazen, sitting in silence, was the portal. I experienced meditation, often talked about as a sitting practice, as a *seeing* practice. What was taught as Zen forms was experienced as connecting with the unseen world through the body.

My sense of Zen as shamanic might have been related to an earlier experience I had within the dharma. Prior to Zen practice, I had engaged in fifteen years of vigorous chanting in the Nichiren Buddhist tradition. I had been chanting a mantra and the teaching of the Lotus Sutra daily for hours. They said, "Chant like your head is on fire," and so I did. It was clear that the practice of concentration, stillness, and silence was to be taken seriously.

After about seven years of chanting, a lucid dream delivered an oracle of healing that would change my life. Prior to the dream, I had many smaller lucid dreams, stimulated by the vigorous chanting, that included forgiving members of my immediate family. I saw the forgiveness dreams as purification of woundedness so that the larger dream, an oracle of wisdom, could come through. I also had many water dreams in which floods inundated my neighborhood and I swam to save folks or myself. I'd wake up short of breath and then remember that I didn't know how to swim.

The night I dreamed of messages that created the oracle, I had an intense headache before going to bed. There was so much pain; I begged out loud, "Please relieve me of this pain and I will serve in the way that I was born to do. Even if I lose everything, I will remain a humble servant."

I hoped the ancestors were listening—or God, or anybody or anything that would ease the pain. Something heard me and accepted my pact of serving humanity.

At 4:00 a.m. the next morning, the pain was gone, but my head was filled with messages and images that made no sense at the time. Later the same morning, I shared the dream with a friend as well as the messages from it that I had written down. I directly asked her, "Where can I get the oracle called the Black Angel Cards?" *Black angels* were the words I heard in the dream. I wasn't interested in angels, black ones or otherwise. My friend was stunned and said that she had not heard of such an oracle. I paced the floor for hours. Something like they show in the movies had happened to me. I wanted to hide. But the friend encouraged me, and I proceeded to create oracle cards transmitted to me by the dream.

I drew the images without knowing how to paint. I wrote down messages that I didn't understand. The oracle card set was eventually published with a large publishing house. The advance paid was so large, it gave me four years to work on the project and deliver it into the world. In the beginning, I saw that this creation was meant particularly for the healing of black women. Over time, it proved to be for all those who felt the pain of oppression. But the birth of the oracle wasn't the full story. Only I knew this. I felt I may have stunted a vast dream into a book and deck of illustrated cards. In trying to extend the healing from my experience of the oracle, had I also adulterated the full extent of that experience—which, for me, was a culmination of years of Buddhist practice?

As I struggled with these questions, I came to see that I

had been kicked into the true vastness of life that could not be concretized. There was only a ghost of my former self and a way of being that I had to leave behind.

* * *

Looking back on my experience that night and in the years that followed, I now see that I came into consciousness of the infinite through a lucid dream while on the path of dharma. A kind of liberation happened despite oppressive systems and life-threatening conditions. I had been receiving information through lucid dreams all my life—why was I only now becoming receptive to it? Chanting and meditating opened a channel between me and the voice of the earth that had been there for years, unacknowledged. It was clear to me that rituals and ceremonies based on the Buddha's teachings carried transformation and healing within them as they opened portals to wisdom. This is the shamanic way of life.

In this writing, I am using the words *shamanic* and *shaman* in a nontraditional way, to illuminate how I see their relationship to Zen. Before I explain what is nontraditional, I want to take a look at how shamanism has traditionally been understood.

The word *shaman* has been lifted from the Tungus language of ancient Mongolia. The root of the word *shaman* originates from *šamán*, which means "to know." To know is not an intellectual process. It is to know the spirit of things, of people, of life—the nature of the unseen world behind our physical world. Etymologists have also noted that the Tungus word may have come from the Chinese word for "Buddhist monk" (*sha men*) via the Sanskrit *sramana*.[6] This latter finding furthers my connection of shamanism with Buddhist practice. Does not a shaman deal with birth, illness, old age, and death? Is not a shaman a bodhisattva, a spiritual warrior, who offers their life to help the sufferer, and the sufferer commits to walking alongside the shaman for well-being?

I experienced shamanic Buddhism on a trip throughout Central Asia with Sakyadhita International Association of Buddhist Women. In Mongolia, our traveling group met a sangha led by married nuns with children. The nuns were all energy healers who used Buddhist rituals and ceremonies. Neighboring communities came to the sangha for healing ailments—physical, mental, and spiritual. In essence, their practices of meditation, chanting, and so forth were used to divine illness through their deep understanding of human nature as espoused by the Buddha. These women were priestesses of magic.

We also visited a thousand-year-old temple of Tibetan monks, who invited us to a ceremony. The one-room temple was lit only by sunlight through small windows. Every space was filled with trinkets and sculptures. Red, yellow, green, blue, and gold colors, although faded, blended with the ornate robes and hats of the monks, who sat in parallel rows across from each other. First, the traditional Chod drums were played by each monk, then the larger drums began. Large cymbals clashed. I must have already been taken by the spirit of the ceremony because I don't remember when the dancers appeared in the aisle between the two rows of monks. As they danced, fully dressed in ceremonial regalia, many of the travelers in our group began to take photos. I felt uncomfortable with the photography but decided to join in documenting the shamanic dance, chanting, and drumming that were occurring. They never instructed us to not take pictures. The reason became clear after I tried to do so. Not one of my photos was clear. There were only streaks of red and green lights—not a face, not a body was captured no matter how many times I focused the lens. The energy conjured would not allow it.

In rural Mongolia, we visited another monastery where thousands of monks had been killed by the reigning Mongolian People's Revolutionary (Communist) Party in an effort to rid the country of Buddhism in the 1930s. Their remains are still buried on the land. There were many shrines to them with blue *katas* (Tibetan offering scarves) flying like flags from poles. There was a shrine that was a small Native American teepee, an affirmation of the ancestral relationship between the Mongolians and the Diné people of North America. Witnessing and experiencing the Mongolian Buddhist culture, in which they use the shamanic energy of Buddha, was what inspired me to pay more attention to the forms of Zen. I sought to know if shamanic bones lay buried in that Buddhist tradition as well.

. ˚ .

The shaman is guided by the forms of this world—by nature. All forms, including ourselves, are of nature, from nature. The forms of the forest, like a hawk or a tree, may be the messenger of wisdom for the shaman. Therefore, the shaman develops a relationship with nature, with all forms including other human beings. Form is the conduit, the connection to wisdom. In Zen, there are many forms through which we come to know the spirit of all things, of life. The spirit of these forms goes beyond zendos and Buddha Halls. Perhaps the forms become dreams and visions for the world.

Shamanism traditionally involves going into an altered state of consciousness and through that state speaking to deities on behalf of one's community. In this text, I am making the case that the practices of chanting, zazen, rituals, and ceremonies can likewise bring altered states of consciousness—though not necessarily ones deep enough to communicate with unseen deities or spirits. I hold that the spirit of the Zen forms is shamanic in bringing us closer to nature and closer to who we are. I see the bones of this way of practice as the ancient tradition of Zen and Buddhism hidden in the earth of India, Mongolia, China, Korea, Japan, Malaysia, Vietnam, and other regions of Asia. Though this writing is meant to share Zen as a portal, it is not about becoming a shaman for personal gain or using Zen practice as a means to an end. It is not to influence you to think in a certain way about Zen practice. It is meant to explore unnamed aspects of the practice in an effort to enhance the significance of its forms, rituals, and ceremonies. Although I quote scholarship from time to time, this writing is not an intellectual or scholarly approach to the topic, but one steeped in experience, inquiry, and exploration. If I have made any mistakes or overgeneralized in any of my arguments about the relationship of Zen to shamanism, I hope that it is outweighed by my efforts to address this large and important topic, which has been largely left unspoken in Zen circles.

In essence, I am speaking of stillness of the mind and body as a different consciousness than that of our everyday busy lives. There is a semi-altered state that opens your life and provides an expansion in such stillness. Over time, the expansion may become more of a shamanic experience in which there is an awakened state of consciousness—something much more vast than the intellectual mind. Shamans are awakened ones who can guide others to awakening.

. * .

Soon after the dream, my life began to change. The pact I had made to be relieved of pain and suffering was being fulfilled—by loss. I was in the middle of a successful career in nonprofit development and community organizing. I had raised millions of dollars for nonprofit organizations, including cofounding the Marcus Garvey School, a private alternative school for black children in Los Angeles. Although I had been trying to "save the world" in this way since childhood, my drive for that work suddenly seemed gone. I had lost my swank apartment in Oakland that folks would say looked straight out of *Architectural Digest* magazine, even though the furniture was mostly used items. (I had a knack for making cheap things look luxurious.) I had lost my new car, and friends left my side one by one for various reasons. I was dumbfounded.

Suddenly, I was thrown into facing more pain, but not mine. As word of the oracle cards spread, I came into being of service to those who suffered, especially black women, creating healing circles all over the country. As a burgeoning seer, I was learning to see into people's lives and to see their ancestors. It was powerful and intense work, and I soon burned out. While I still had my beautiful home, I felt stuck there, in constant tears. My Buddhist practice suffered in the transition from being a regular civilian into an intuitive. I would later discover, a few years into my Zen practice, that ancient Zen priests were seers, and the sangha or community came to the temple for their guidance. But I did not have that sense of tradition or structure at that time.

The card deck and my intuitive gift were confirmed by many seers and mediums of the unseen world, but I did not know how to integrate what had happened to me. I sat in the world feeling alone and lost. Even though I had promised to work for the wellness of humanity and was being offered a way to serve that I never could have imagined, I felt uncomfortable with the "mini-fame" that began growing around me, the folks that wanted me to save them. I stayed with the confusion. In the end, it was clear the deck came through the gateway of my dharma practice to save me by bringing understanding of the nature of life. This was a necessary step for me to fulfill the pact of helping to save humanity; I was to continue easing the suffering of injustice within and without.

·°·

While walking *kinhin* (walking meditation) in a Zen center on a hot day, I realized that I had set aside the Black Angel oracle until such time as I understood the nature of my own heart and mind. I also realized I had left my Nichiren Buddhist community of fifteen years. I moved on from the deep concentration practice of the Nichiren tradition without making a conscious decision to leave. It just happened—in the same way I never had a desire to know Buddha or Buddhism and never made a conscious effort to know such but was led right there by ancestors.

Sadness overwhelmed the choice my heart was making. I chose an increase in silence over the constant chanting of the mantra Nam-Myoho-Renge-Kyo.

I chose to stop and look at what had happened in my life with the dreaming and the chanting that led to it. I chose the dark cave of Zen, with its new yet similar kind of chanting. What did the practice of seeing through Buddha's eyes have that led to such a powerful dream? I began a Lakota way of singing and drumming my prayers. What was this new/old self as a seer? How could this happen in the middle of practicing the teachings of Buddha? Would I have to hide this talent in the Buddhist tradition, as I must have been doing most of my life?

The nature of the true self is exposed in Zen practice. This I would experience as I continued walking, hands folded in *shashu*, around the zendo with other aspirants, day after day. The capacity to see what was in front of me was strengthened in silent meditation. The more I sat in the silence, a deeper silence appeared, and I began to hear messages similar to those that brought forth the oracle deck. It was as if Buddha, a great ancestor, was whispering to me all-day long. I needed the guidance after experiencing such a major dream and transformation, so I listened. I knew no elders of the way of seeing. There was no training for me to go and sit with my ancestral gift, no way to hone the medicine. So, I sat silently in the cave of a dark zendo and was fed and watched over. I would listen to dharma teachers from whom I could feel their seeing practice revealing wisdom from beneath the earth, the place from which Buddha drew his teachings.

I longed for a community of seers, but they were not easy

to access. I longed for a teacher of seers but eventually was told there is none other than oneself. I held my gift close to my chest, conducting some divinations as requested. But mostly I spent the next twenty years in the practice of Zen. There I created a daily devotion to things unseen, to the spirit world, feeling joined in altered states of consciousness. I did not speak of these things while in training, and neither did anyone else.

There is a custom in Zen of learning through observation and imitation rather than by receiving verbal instruction. I understand why the tradition does not openly teach the rituals and ceremonies to those who haven't been trained to receive such profound protocols. Yet I felt something else too—Zen communities were leaning away from Zen as shamanic for fear of being mistaken for new age, witchcraft, or Vodou. In a world with a supermarket of spirituality, with much syncretism and many teachings that borrow from different ancient traditions, I understood Zen communities' desire for clarity, and I also saw their need to simplify the practice so that it fit into the daily life of the general population in the West. But I wondered if this leaning away from what seemed magical or mystical affected the full transmission of Zen to Westerners from the first Zen masters who entered this country.

Were the shamanic bones beneath the practice purposely hidden by the Zen masters from Asia, for fear of the ancient not being taken seriously in a country where the dominant religion was Christianity and where magic was taboo? Did the Zen masters distrust the new seekers, who might misunderstand and even abuse the shamanic aspects of the tradition? Were they protecting the medicine?

I believe that there are Eastern perspectives on the rituals and ceremonies of Zen that have not been transmitted to the West. Without the full and complete transmission, we are left in the middle of the road, so to speak. There is more to our development as seers in a seeing practice. A saying in Zen communities is, "Zazen is good for nothing," meaning you are not looking to gain. However, you are looking, you are seeing, deep into life. You are taking on a seeing practice to discern, or can I say *divine*, life. This is done to bring forth wisdom as a way to attend to suffering, personally and collectively.

What would happen if we were to treat Buddhism as the shamanic practice that it is? I believe the way the practice is transmitted might be different. Rather than create what we *think* is peace, harmony, oneness, and the like, we would relate to the tradition as a path in which to *experience* the absolute truths of life.

Although I focus on Zen in this book, this inquiry pertains more broadly to many Buddhist traditions, and perhaps to the religion as a whole. Sam van Schaik, in his scholarly book *Buddhist Magic: Divination, Healing, and Enchantment Through the Ages*, says, "Despite the importance of magical practices in Buddhism, they are still one of the least studied aspects of the religion. I suspect that one of the main reasons for this is the idealized image of Buddhism as a rational religion, essentially free from superstition and ritual." He goes on to say, "The exclusion of magical practices and powers from most discussions of Buddhism in the modern era can be seen as appropriation of Buddhism by Europeans and

Americans, and also as a result of modernization movements in Asia and within Asian Buddhism."[7] He also writes about the magic in Buddhism being uprooted by elite sects.

Specific to Zen, T. Griffith Foulk writes, "The imputation of a 'denial of ritual,' I conclude, was a strategy employed by scholars to shield the Zen tradition from charges leveled against Buddhism as a whole in late nineteenth and early twentieth-century Japan and China, to wit, that it was a superstitious religion mired in mumbo-jumbo, and that it was antithetical to a scientific world-view and the advance of modern civilization."[8] As noted above, Foulk's essay explores the modern historical construction of a version of Zen without the need for magical rituals and ceremonies, rejecting these as irrelevant to awakening.

Despite these efforts to suppress or remove what I am calling the shamanic aspect of Zen, we do not have to go far to discover the healing and magical roots of the practice. These have remained despite the denial that there is a need for them. We can simply begin to recognize the shamanic bones within what *has* been transmitted in Zen practice. In my experience, it became clear to me that chanting, zazen, rituals, and ceremonies, if taken seriously, can strengthen the process of becoming fully who we are against all odds. Just like Buddha, we can be seers of injustice, seers of illness, and seers of old age and death. You neither need to know upon entering Zen practice the traditional beliefs or intentions nor the liturgies, invocations, or the use of ceremonial objects. So too do you not need to become a magician, healer, or shaman of Zen. You simply come.

In indigenous spiritual practices, including the Buddhist ones that have remained close to the earth, the rituals and ceremonies are meant to draw the ancestors close, to support the prayers, and to guide those who are suffering toward wellness. Unlike many ceremonies of other Buddhist schools, in Zen the task of turning toward wellness or transformation is not a stated intention or necessarily a goal of rituals or ceremonies. With the lack of such explicit intentions, the significance of Zen forms, rituals, and ceremonies might feel lost and can make them seem routine, habitual, and hollow. I have witnessed the boredom, and even the suffering, some Zen students go through in making offerings and participating in ceremonies. Many do not have the patience with the slow and invisible effects of these activities on one's life. To see the impact of shamanic or awakening experiences through ritual and ceremony on our personal and collective lives can take decades. Are we ready to expand our walk on the Buddha Way? Is it time to loosen the dogma and embrace the forms as the bones of Zen from its Eastern origin?

* * *

Once at breakfast in a cafe, with my teacher sitting nearby, I said that Vodou and Zen were the same. One of my teacher's eyebrows moved up her forehead a few inches. I looked away. One of my friends who had come along for the breakfast asked what I meant. I waited. I needed to see if I should censor myself since my teacher was sitting there. But it was too late. Why in the world did I say what I said? I knew the ancestors of Vodou had been trying to reach me since my teenage years. They wanted me to take a seat along with other African diviners. At the age of nineteen, a tribe from Dahomey (a precolonial kingdom located in present-day

Benin) invited me back "home" to take my seat as a diviner. They said I was one of them. Out of fear, I did not go.

While eating my breakfast, I sensed a bit of regret still lingering inside me. Even though I wore the Zen black robe of liberation, I couldn't let the ancestors down by not answering my friend's question about Vodou and Zen. I responded, "Understanding the nature of life is the work of Vodou." I said no more. Two days later, an ordained Zen priest whom I did not know contacted me by email. The email contained words like "Zen priest" and "Vodou practitioner." She was contacting me on behalf of a *mambo* (high priestess of Vodou) in Haiti who had read an essay I wrote. The inner connection between Zen and Vodou had been affirmed in less than forty-eight hours!

The notion of a more esoteric way of Zen life was again affirmed some years after I had been ordained. Hoitsu Suzuki Roshi, the son of the late Shunryu Suzuki Roshi (founder of the San Francisco Zen Center), arrived from Japan for a memorial ceremony for his sister. We were all stationed in our places in the Buddha Hall. Dignitaries of Zen from Japan and across the United States were there. Hoitsu Roshi began to speak to his translator. Suddenly, the front row of teachers was in a bit of chaos. It was a standing ceremony, and the norm is to stand upright and silent. I looked toward Hoitsu Roshi. From where I stood with the priests in the second row, I witnessed him pull out a small black lacquer box. He spoke in Japanese in an adamant voice and was motioning for someone to place the black box on the altar. There was confusion, as this was not part of the rehearsal for the ceremony. Placing this black box on the altar had not been written down in the center's book for memorials.

It felt as if the ceremony was taken hold by the old ways carried by Hoitsu Roshi and his ancestors. I smiled at the commotion, intuiting that he was adding to the ceremony something that had not been transmitted to us Westerners. It was something ancient and unknown.

The Roshi's interpreter opened the black box and then immediately closed it. Time was passing, and everyone knows that everything in Zen is on time and not in time. The interpreter motioned Hoitsu Roshi to put the box on the altar. Finally, there was calm in the room except for a few chuckles from those who saw the exchange between the Roshi and his interpreter as comical. I couldn't wait until the ritual was over. I had a firm plan to run over and find out about the black box. I sensed it had something to do with a deep shamanic practice that connected Zen to its Japanese cultural roots.

After the ceremony, I made my way over to the dining room, pushing past folks so I could get a seat at the table reserved for the Japanese. This was totally out of protocol, but I couldn't help myself. I knew that Hoitsu Roshi had information of the esoteric kind. I asked the interpreter to ask the Roshi if I may talk with him about the box. The Japanese guests had barely taken their seats. Several members of Hoitsu Roshi's family bowed and invited me to sit down with them. I felt a bit selfish because the guests, numbering at least ten, had not even been served their lunch. But it was probably fascinating for them to have the only black priest at the ceremony sit with them, so they could get a better look. Maybe my presence also gave them a sense of being part of the whole rather than separated at a table by themselves.

I arranged my robes as nicely as possible, looked into the

Roshi's face, and asked, "Please tell me. What was in the box?" His eyes lit up with enthusiasm. He asked the interpreter to hand him the box. Slowly, the food was coming to the table. It didn't stop the Roshi from opening the box. He pulled out a tiny bundle, unwrapped a piece of linen, and placed in my hands what looked like a dried dead worm. He began speaking in Japanese as I held it. He grinned with excitement. The interpreter said that I was holding a piece of the umbilical cord that had connected Roshi's sister and their mother at the time of the sister's birth. It is a tradition to preserve the umbilical cord and place it on the altar during memorials upon the death of the children, regardless of their age at the time of death. It is to honor the matriarchal lineage. In many homes in Japan, there are numerous small black boxes on the altar. I felt myself between tears and nausea, holding the piece of umbilical cord that was cut from the newborn body of the Roshi's sister, many decades before her death. This experience was a major turning point in my spiritual life. I felt that a door had opened to begin exploring the integration of my innate seer capacity and my practice of Zen.

Within the sangha that I lead, the rituals and ceremonies are crucial. I can espouse my views about oppression and internalized oppression, but it is the rituals of Zen, clear of my thinking and conceptualization, that will give my students an *experience* of liberation despite oppression. I am merely the conduit that encourages aspirants of awakening to continue sitting, seeing, bowing, and offering themselves, also, as conduits of wisdom. In ritual, aspirants are not following me, the person, as much as following and witnessing a way to take action, with attention, in the midst of their suffering. Every student must contend with the question: do you feel controlled by the rituals, or are they leading you in silence to the place of compassion and insight?

Ceremonies of all kinds have been a profound part of my life. In my experience, the rituals are fueled through their interconnection with everyone and everything during ceremony. Ceremony in the context of this writing means a gathering of rituals or forms into a shared activity—a dynamic activity that collectively embodies wisdom teachings. It is a communal sharing of oneself as part of the prayer, so to speak, as a devotee to awakening along with others. In Zen ceremony, a world outside of our usual world is created to enhance devotion and provide an immersive experience of silent action that is transformative and potentially beneficial to collective action in the world. It was during these ceremonies, in the early years of my Zen practice, that I experienced altered states of consciousness amid intense collective energy. I felt to be no-self, in its truest sense, which is to be interconnected to everything and everyone—whether I wanted to or not. A bell, a whisk, the smell of incense, the drum, the hand that passes the offerings—these things cannot be done with the limitations of the mind. To think of yourself doing it alone, and how perfect or imperfect you are, overshadows the act of being. In being, the role of the rituals and the ceremony can bring you closer to the source by which your life came into being. There is no container in the hard, limited sense. There is only water by which you can float or drown, live or die—either way can be experienced as healing and transformative.

While I refer often in this book to ritual and ceremony, drawing on my experience as a Zen practitioner and dharma transmitted teacher, I do not explicitly provide the actual rituals, ceremonies, or secret chants used by transmitted teachers in particular ceremonies of Soto Zen. The transmission of these practices must be led by those trained and authorized, and in an appropriate setting. The content is sacred and cannot be understood out of context. Even in context, it would be overwhelming for teachers to first explain the reasons for the tools and incantations before every ritual or ceremony. Rituals and ceremonies are to be lived. Your own bones must be rattled. It would be a waste of time to give details to something you cannot understand with the mind. However, I think it may help wedge open what feels mysterious about Zen activity, and is often misunderstood, especially to those starting out in Zen practice. I share only as far as to reveal and enliven a dimension of Zen that is rarely discussed yet is so beneficial in understanding the kind of transformation occurring within the practice. Zen ritual and ceremony also help explain the tradition's stark difference from secular practices of meditation and mindfulness. The most important teaching for me to share is that not only does Zen occur within but also for the benefit of all.

I'm neither fascinated with myself nor do I have the need to embellish my capacities as a seer. I am more interested in how a deep samadhi and consistently sitting in silence enhances the intuitive nature of being, awakens the infinite, and furthers the field of illumination. I am interested in the expansiveness of Zen practice and how we might include more ancient Zen traditions in our contemporary Western practice. By incorporating other aspects of Zen, especially shamanic ones, we can live in time and space without beginning or end. The veil can be lifted on who we are as living beings. We can relax the mind. We don't need to figure everything out. In a shamanic way, we can allow the practice to work on us rather than working the practice. A wider perspective on the teachings will ripen our transmissions and return us to the earth, to the root of all religions and spiritual paths.

. ° .

In my life, an inner temple was revealed in chanting and meditation. It tied together my dreams, deep intuition, and a natural inclination toward Zen as a way of life. In my experience of the rituals, ceremonies, and forms for more than twenty years, I have been led to an indescribable connection to the infinite. It brings mysticism and meditation together into a place of wholeness. Zen, for me, has something to do with using the physicality of life—to use form, which is to use the body, to experience the unseen and invisible dimensions of life.

Many will not agree with this exploration I am presenting. I have no choice. I came to Zen with my eyes open, never to be shut again. When the candles are lit in the zendo, the incense is offered, and the bows to ancestors are made, I cannot help but honor what the earth reveals—a divine Zen.

Preparing
the Sanctuary
for Ritual

In the dark early morning while aspirants are still sleeping, I slip downstairs to perform the ritual before ringing the wake-up bell. I bow to the han, a wooden drum hanging on a rope. One beat with the mallet. I bow again. I go down a few stairs and bow to a handbell sitting on a small shelf. I carry it with me into the dark zendo. Both hands are wrapped around the bell's handle, at the center of my body near my heart. I walk and bow to the altar upon which sits Manjushri, the god of wisdom, who cuts through darkness. I ring the bell in a cascading motion, up and down, three times. I bow again and step to the left and walk to the nearest corner. I ring the bell in that corner. I go to the next corner and ring the bell. I go to the next and the next. I am waking up the spirits of the sanctuary, letting the ancestors know we are coming. I am clearing the energy of the space where the ritual of zazen will take place. I bow again at the altar and ring the bell three times in a cascading rhythm, as it has been done for centuries.

In every ceremony, the place—land, circle, house, or temple—must be cleansed before the people enter. It is important that the people are also cleansed before participating in the healing ritual. This cleansing may be washing of the feet and hands before entering the sanctuary. I have witnessed the cleansing of the land with those who practice the Lakota Way. They place burning coals in a large can and add the needles of a cedar tree to induce the fragrance of the earth.

Those selected to do the cleansing use the smoke first to cleanse themselves and pray. Then, lightly swinging their cans with the smoke, the selected walk the ceremonial land, cleansing much like how Catholic priests smoke the cathedral by swinging a cauldron of frankincense.

Instead of swinging a pot of smoke, in the Zen center, a bell, much like a Christmas bell, is rung in a cascading rhythm to energetically clear the space for zazen. In each case, the spiritual act of cleansing is done to rid the ritual space of unseen things that might interrupt the ceremony. The first time I rang the bell in the four corners of the zendo, the meditation hall, it was exactly like what I had seen in African traditions wherein people clear the space in the four corners of the house with smoking sage leaves and rattles before a ceremony. I had done this same ritual many times in my own home. The ringing of the bells in the zendo vibrated inside me as the shamanic bones of Zen.

. . .

Sanctuary space is important to the success of rituals and ceremonies. The design and texture of the sanctuary play a role in protection from interference with sacred activities. The sanctuary must provide calm and tranquility, which is the reason many rituals and ceremonies are held in remote places in nature. Upon entering the sanctuary, a participant's shoulders should fall, and a naturally inward gaze should come upon them.

The Zen sanctuary is designed and ready for the life of Zen, which is full of rituals and ceremonies. Altars are built throughout the temple, with different tutelary figures on each of them. In larger sanctuaries, the Buddha sits on the altar of the Buddha Hall, where chanting is traditionally practiced and where ordinations and other ceremonies take place. Manjushri, holding a sword to cut away illusion, oversees the zendo. Avalokiteshvara or Guan Yin, the bodhisattva of compassion, is certain to grace another altar. There are many iconic figures, and each represents certain virtues to live by. The Rinzai Zen teacher and poet Hakuin (1686–1768) said, "Make the whole universe your own personal meditation cave."[1] This gives us freedom in creating sanctuary for Zen practice.

A sanctuary can be as simple as a humble hut that evokes a place of peace. In "Song of the Grass Hut," an eighth-century poem, Shitou (700–790) describes the creation of a space that fosters just sitting. He says, "Though the hut is small, it includes the entire world."[2] Shitou presents a simple environment and a simple way to just sit, yet it is still within a created sanctuary. The hut includes the entire world, the entire earth, or the entire universe.

In modern times, where Zen rituals and ceremonies take place tends to be far more than a hut. Each Zen center varies. Some centers operate out of homes. Some make do with rental spaces, setting up temporary altars and rows of cushions in yoga studios or storefronts. Others have been created in the same style as the ancient Zen monasteries of China. These display an elaborate physical layout in which each room in the monastery hosts certain rituals and ceremonies. Each has great functional importance, as particular rituals occur in them at certain times. The zendo and Buddha Hall are where the most important sacred activities occur. But the consecration of sanctuary space occurs even in the kitchen, hallways, and dining hall, where daily rituals of chanting and bowing take place.

The sanctuary is more than just a building or space intended for ceremony or ritual. It is also a part of the larger community where it resides, and so the appearance of the sanctuary affects a wider field of beings. This has always been true: in ancient China and Japan, notwithstanding political misuse of religious power, temples and monasteries were placed in provinces to support harmony and peace in society. In many cases, the temples were commissioned works of art that became proud landmarks within a community.

In essence, the sanctuary goes beyond its walls. It can act as a symbol of peace. I remember, when practicing Nichiren Buddhism in San Francisco, one of our temples was placed near a large park where there had been drug use and gang activity. A year later, neighbors came to share gratitude for the center because its presence had changed the activity in the park, making it feel safe once more. When I created a Zen center, I chose one of the busiest streets in East Oakland, where I lived, for its location. I expressed in form what Zen felt like to me. I wanted the temple to be in the middle of the chaos, to serve as an oasis, to affect all those who lived near. Not everyone came for meditation, but folks came by to thank us for creating the center in the neighborhood. We saw immigrant Chinese neighbors, who never said a word to us, voluntarily taking care of the plants out front that we planted in honor of Buddha. The temple didn't survive, but I am certain its existence left a mark on the hearts of those living near.

The sanctuary's physical existence as sacred space mirrors the earth with its smells, light, food, flowers, grass tatami mats, wood, and stone statues. Every person is a Zen temple; every temple is Shitou's hut. When we take care of ourselves, we take care of the sanctuary. Simultaneously, when we take care of the earth, we take care of humanity, because we are the earth. So, when we enter the sanctuary, we enter ourselves, we bow to our lives, and we make offerings from the earth before we take a seat upon it.

∴

Before moving on from the topic of preparing sanctuary, I want to address the issue of hierarchy in such spaces—its use and misuse.

In a traditional Japanese-style zendo or Buddha Hall, seating is hierarchically arranged, according to position and seniority. Although I understand the traditional nature of the hierarchy, I have witnessed how the roles can be treated as positions of power over the ritual participants, used to police the accuracy of others' ceremonial performance. When I consider Buddhist ritual from a shamanic standpoint, the hierarchy appears to have a different purpose in the sanctuary.

In Soto Zen group meditation, it is common that participants face toward the wall in emulation of Bodhidharma, the sage monk from India who founded the Zen (Ch'an) lineage in China. Abbots and former abbots, as well as those in active teaching roles, do not face the wall but rather face out toward the assembly. I remember, during my first time co-leading an *ango* (a traditional ninety-day Zen practice period), facing out during the ritual of zazen. In my position as one of the teachers/guides of the ritual, I experienced this facing out as taking care of the participants, sensing whether they were doing well or not. The sensing was not done by actively looking around, as I too was in zazen. The caretaking required a deep sensing or intuition honed over the years from just sitting. As one of the "holders" in the sanctuary, I felt as though I was assisting in creating an experience of the environment as the whole universe. This seems to me like the intended function of hierarchy in shamanic ritual—as holders and guides rather than enforcers of protocol.

Once the bell rings, the ritual ends and the entire assembly lets go of their posture. Then the crossover from ritual—leaving the zendo—tends to bring another form of hierarchy. This too can entail a distorted power over the participants if there is not a consciousness that the ritual of zazen must be continued as the foundation to all other actions. Once we cross out of the threshold of the ritual of zazen, we can slip into a state of being that clashes with the effects of the rituals and ceremonies. If the structure of hierarchy in the sanctuary matches the structure of the organizational hierarchy, this can cause confusion regarding the purpose of rituals and ceremonies. It can seem as if the purpose of the temple and aspirants is to support the hierarchy whereas, in truth, the purpose of the hierarchy is to support those who are participating. If the positions in the sanctuary are closely tied to being caretakers of the participants, the oppressive tendencies that emerge in sustaining the organization can be eased, if not lifted. In this way, the spirit of Zen is maintained and felt throughout every activity including the "work" of the institution.

Ultimately, sanctuary is within. We walk spiritual paths by gathering ways of living that are in alignment with peace. Outer sanctuaries help us in doing so. When we are in a spiritual community, perfect or not, we see ourselves more clearly. We see the depth of our pain and rage while bowing or offering incense and flowers. We move so slowly that what is in our bodies cannot be overlooked. At first, we might feel self-conscious in a community that observes our human frailty. Over time, the ritual and ceremony take center stage and you begin to see another side of yourself, another side of life, despite being human. This side of life goes unseen in the rush of daily living. Creating sanctuary within requires the practice of stillness and silence provided in outer sanctuaries. When we get a glimpse of the unseen, we are brought back from where we emerged—be it the earth or the source of all life.

Making Offerings
to the Ancestors

Candles are lit and placed on altars that have been prepared beforehand, laid with fine cloth upon which to receive the offerings. The rice and tea are carried in red lacquer cups and trays. Each person in the procession holds a tower of offerings at the heart, their hands positioned on either side of the tray. The offerings are aligned so as to make a picture of palms joined in reverence. The hands are connected to the offering. The hands are to give and to receive. The offering is raised over the bowed head of the receiver, the teacher, the one who has embodied the teachings for decades, as the offering to Buddha is one's whole life.

For eons across spiritual, cultural, and religious traditions, people have made offerings in honor of ancestors. It is a critical step before partaking in any ritual or ceremony. In essence, the people, teachings, and the land that have sustained the wisdom tradition are to be honored prior to the activities in which the spiritual community will participate, heal, and transform. Making offerings to ancestors is a wordless expression of devotion to awakening and an acknowledgment of the earth that supports us.

When making offerings, the persons making them also receive what is given. For example, offering water may bring a calm mind, flowers a sense of beauty. Incense helps connect you to the earth, while firelit candles create illumination and symbolize destroying the darkness of ignorance. Inherent in each offering is a simultaneous giving and receiving of these gifts.

Perhaps you have been to a ceremony based on indigenous traditions. In each case, there are altars that hold the symbols of the teachings and honor ancestors. For example, in the many ceremonies I participated in with seers of the Vodou tradition from Dahomey, Africa, there was always a huge altar in honor of the beloved ancestors. All the elements that sustain our lives were present: a large fire to satisfy and receive the ancestors; their favorite foods, sweets, and liquor; and cigars or other forms of tobacco. All of these were offered so that the singing, drumming, and dancing would be received, and the prayers would be lifted into the atmosphere.

In many indigenous cultures, making offerings is an exchange for wellness and ridding one's life of evil doings or obstacles. Making offerings is a way to embody nature and the teachings that come from nature. For example, in the Lakota Way ceremonies that I participated in, altars were made on the ground from the soil of the land. They served as a place to bring the bones and skins of animal ancestors, viewed as medicine. And they held the *chanupas* (pipes), which were filled with the prayers of those who danced on behalf of the community. Medicines of the earth such as sage, sweetgrass, and cedar were infused with prayer and offered in turn to the ancestors and to the participants of the ceremony.

I was introduced to rituals and symbolic offerings in the black Christian church of my childhood. While we didn't call it ritual, my African sensibility knew it to be such. The altar was filled with the symbols of Christ's blood and body—grape juice for blood and leaven crackers for the body.

As the Sunday service came to an end, our bodies would commune with the body of Christ through ingesting the food and drink. This is similar to many Christian churches, including the Catholic tradition where there is communion, incense, singing, and chanting.

. • .

Central to the ceremonial life of most, if not all, Buddhist traditions are ritual offerings to ancestors. Food, flowers, water, incense, rice, sweets, tea, sculpted offerings, and other significant items are given to invoke and honor the ancestors of the lineage or school.

At Zen temples and monasteries, it is a daily practice to give gratitude for the inheritance that has sustained the teachings, the sangha, and one's life. Prior to the opening of the morning sitting and service, offerings of incense or flowers are made at various altars throughout the temple and temple grounds. This is done just before dawn while the aspirants are seated in silence. Commonly the teacher makes offerings on their behalf, and this is the reason it is important to arrive early to the zendo. The heart of the teacher, the heart of the aspirants, and the offerings come together in ceremony to honor the ancestors and the teachings. If one is sick and can't come to the zendo, then energetically receiving the offerings from bed is most important to recovering and returning to the daily ceremonies for the whole of one's life and the community.

Although the dailiness of rituals of offering was part of what attracted me to Zen, I have come to see that repetition comes with its own risks. At times, it can feel there is more attention to routine rather than reverence of making offerings to ancestors—ancestors of the East as well as the ancestors of all who are dedicating their lives to awakening. The teaching is to bring one's whole life and whole heart to the path. Such giving of one's life is symbolic of the actual sacrifices historically found in many spiritual and religious traditions, including the sacrifice of Jesus Christ to save humanity, the piercing of flesh as an offering in Lakota Sundance ceremonies, or the sacrifices of animals in many indigenous sacred rites.

The Zen tradition contains a number of its own such stories. The Chinese monk Huineng (638–713) offered his life when he discovered his teacher, Hongren (601–674), was dying. Huineng felt that he should die before his teacher and so made a gesture of self-sacrifice in hopes to sustain the teacher and the teachings for as long as possible. In the end, he became the successor of Hongren's esoteric teachings as found in the Platform Sutra.

Another famous Zen story of offering one's life is that of a Chinese monk named Huike (487–593). A celebrated scholar, he abandoned the intellectual knowing of Zen to become a monk. His desire to experience the depth of the teachings was so great, he begged Bodhidharma, the great teacher who had come from India to China, to take him on as a student. Huike sat outside for many days in the snow, pleading each day for Bodhidharma to become his teacher. Eventually, Huike cut his arm off to demonstrate the seriousness of his intentions. Upon the act of sacrificing an arm, he was accepted as Bodhidharma's first disciple. Years later, Bodhidharma asked Huike what he had attained. Huike simply bowed in silence, revealing his understanding of Bodhidharma's wordless teachings. Huike then received the great transmission of the Lankavatara Sutra, Buddha's teachings of self-realization that had been passed down through the ages.

Whether or not Huike actually cut off his arm or suffered in the snow for days and survived these grave situations, the story makes clear that entering a path of Zen requires commitment from the depth of one's whole life, giving the whole heart in order to experience the wordless expression of life. While there is no offering of the literal body as a sacrifice in Zen ceremony and ritual, one is offering oneself, symbolically, for the sake of awakening—the shamanic experience.

Seen against this background of bodily sacrifice and wholehearted commitment, it becomes clear that, in Zen, the daily offerings of rice, incense, tea, flowers, chants, and candlelight are symbolic of the body, which is symbolic of the earth. To make offerings to ancestors, to awakened ones, to wisdom holders who have come before us, is to bring that wisdom forth into our lives. In making offerings to ancestors, we are acknowledging all that came before us including plants, trees, four-legged animals, winged ones, and those who live in water. Making offerings is an act of spirit through our bodies. We are not *doing* something; we are being led to an alignment with the unseen, suchness, the unexpressible, and the unsurpassable.

.＊.

To honor all life through collective ritual attends to our collective suffering, despite and because of our differences. Making offerings has persisted despite and because of poverty, illness, insurmountable death, corruption, and all the other devastations that afflict humanity. Ancient African warriors made sacrifices and offerings to sustain their medicine and the wisdom needed to survive. Even in the midst of wars, the Japanese warrior clan, the samurai, laid down their armor at the door of the monastery. There they made offerings to the ancestors, chanted, and bowed, knowing a connection to the earth and ancestors would be necessary whether they won or lost, lived or died.

It was a profound experience for me, as a spiritual warrior, to offer incense at Zen altars in the midst of oppression. Offering incense to the ancestors through my own body, I experienced compassion and love for life while suffering. It was clear I didn't have to wait for suffering to end, that I was being taught to take spiritual action in the face of inevitable human conditioning. This is important to those who suffer outside of the dominant culture with a lack of resources or attention to their well-being.

We do not make offerings to ancestors for our own sake. We make offerings for our families and communities, through our bodies. Others are inherently with us, as we would not be on the planet without them.

Ancestors are everyone and everything that existed on the planet before your birth. Ancestors can include the earth, moon, sun, and stars. They can include the people in your blood lineage (loved or unloved). Included are those whom we want to disown because we feel they did not walk with integrity or were harmful to others. Their "wrongful actions" have something to do with how we personally and collectively live, and they too are ancestors. Ancestors are also people in the lineage of your spiritual practice, and beings in the lineage of life itself.

All spiritual and religious paths are ancestral. Buddhism is an ancestral practice in which the Buddha is the most revered ancestor. This is why offerings from the earth are made to his teachings. The Buddha knew himself to be in a stream of ancestors, also known as Buddhas. There were Buddhas before the one Buddha who is exalted today.

When we bring in the ancestors at the beginning of a ritual or ceremony, we are starting with the bones. The bones, in this writing, are symbolic of wisdom. In some indigenous cultures, bones are said to hold memory. It is not our brains that hold the remembrance of human life before our births. The memories in the bones can be stirred or rattled, as they say, through ritual and ceremony. Through our bones, we can access wisdom that has been passed from ancestors to the present. Don't archeologists look to the bones of people from ancient cultures to discover stories about those who lived before our time? Since life throughout time is marked on the bones, it is certain that we hold the past; the wisdom of the past is within us.

The bones of Zen include the stories, culture, and tradition of those who have walked the path for thousands of years. I placed this chapter, "Making Offerings to the Ancestors," toward the beginning of this book on purpose. I wanted to acknowledge that I am writing from their bones—from a place deeper than my own rational thoughts. When I say my bones are rattled in Zen rituals and ceremonies, I am saying that a deep knowing comes through in tears, a knowing of myself as something beyond physical existence. I often do not know the reason for the tears or chills other than the sweetness that comes with bowing, chanting, and making offerings. Therefore, I make offerings slowly and with breath, to allow what needs to come through for the benefit of all. In the process, I remember through my bones the ancient way of ritual and ceremony. I never would have thought Zen practice could bring tears. But my bones knew something I didn't.

Honoring Zen Ancestors

Whose bones do we acknowledge in communal Zen ceremonies? In the chanting service that takes place every morning at Zen monasteries and temples, aspirants chant a long list of the names of ancestors from India, China, and Japan. When chanting these names, we are honoring those who upheld the teachings that opened doors to awakening throughout time. We are making a connection to the ancient teachings that were embodied in them and perhaps now live in our bones.

Today, many people engage Zen practice without any acknowledgment to the ancestors of the tradition. Not acknowledging them creates a separation from those who brought us this practice of awakening. In the disconnection, the act of making offerings can become routinized, losing its significance and heart. The collective action of awakening is lost.

Perhaps one aspect of this disconnection is ethnic or racial. Whether from a sense of superiority, inadequacy, or self-consciousness, some of us energetically or literally separate ourselves from the act of making offerings because of not being Japanese, Chinese, Vietnamese, or Korean. Many who are not Asian have practiced Zen for decades, without regard to the people and the land from where the teachings emerged. Embracing Zen without taking steps to honor the bones of the ancestors in the lineage is a form of appropriation. When we ignore the bones, we appropriate. With appropriation, we don't see the practice as one of enhancing interrelationship but one of personal improvement. We don't recognize the bones of Zen practice as embodying true connection among us. And we don't see that there is an opportunity in ritual and ceremony to activate justice through collective awakening with the help of ancestors or who or what were here before our birth.

Buddhism arose from the flames of suffering among the people of India. It emerged from the suffering Buddha saw among his Shakya people—the poor, the aged, those dying from neglect, and all those he felt needed the kind of liberation that he discovered. It is important to remember that ritual and ceremony arose in Buddhism because it was the way an ancient people attended to their suffering.

. ° .

None of my blood ancestors are Chinese or Japanese, as far as I know. I could have easily walked into Zen and denied any connection to East Asian people, but I did not. I was aware of being of African descent participating in a practice from the earth of Japan. I was once reprimanded by another black person for being of African descent and following a practice rooted in Asia. I did not have an immediate response to her concern. Over time, however, I have come to acknowledge the loss of a historical kinship between Asians and black people of African descent. Due to the East African slave trade and then voluntary immigration, those from premodern and modern Africa contributed to the history and culture of India, Turkey, Pakistan, China, and many other Asian countries. In my bones, I felt this ancestral connection when I heard the chants and the bell-ringing of Buddhist practice.

Some years after the woman confronted me about being a black person practicing Buddhism, I met a seer from Ghana who told me of my connection to ancient Chinese people. She asked me to create and perform a ritual to support Chinese people. I had made many offerings to African ancestors but never to any from another continent. While I felt connected to Chinese and Japanese people even before I entered Buddhist practice, I had never made offerings to these ancestors outside of Buddhist ritual. I had not honored my connection to those who brought Buddhism to the United States and relied on it to survive their experiences of discrimination and dehumanization.

I did as the seer asked of me. I let the unknown lead in creating the ritual for the ancestors of my practice, whether they practiced Buddhism or not. I went to Chinatown in Oakland and gathered Chinese toys, teas, food, and treats for my unknown Chinese ancestors. I was led by my heart to do the ritual in West Oakland, where black people from Louisiana and Texas had been living since the 1940s and where the train tracks had been laid down by Chinese immigrants in the 1860s. I had assistance from a dear friend who often accompanied me on these special journeys. At 10:00 p.m., we stood in the middle of the street, next to railroad tracks, and I laid out my offerings, chanted, and prayed. When I grew dizzy, it was clear to me that the work was done. I jumped back into the car, realizing that I should have done such a thing years ago.

Verifying the existence of early contacts between Africans and Buddhists is difficult. We know that most enslaved

Africans in Asia converted not to Buddhism but to Islam. Yet religious interchange was an important element of cultural exchange, and I suspect there was crossover of spiritual practices between East Indians and Africans, creating a historical connection between Africans and Buddhism.

I am glad that the person asked about my participation in an Asian practice as a black person. She stimulated a quest for understanding and connection that continues each time I bow. The act of making offerings in my Zen practice, with the wisdom of the bones of its ancestors, creates expansion and nurtures the physical and spiritual interrelationships of Zen, then and now. Another expansion for me has been to explore the use of the term *ancestors* in place of the more common Zen term, *patriarchs*.

From Patriarchs to Ancestors

Zen ancestors are traditionally called "patriarchs," and so perhaps, it is not surprising that we find patriarchy in the practice. In Zen centers in Japan and the United States, people traditionally chanted a lineage that included only those who are considered male (some still do). More recently, however, a host of transmitted Zen teachers have researched and brought in to Zen centers chanting a lineage of women ancestors. It begins with the women in Buddha's family: his aunt Mahaprajapati, who raised him; Mitta, his mother-in-law; and Yasodhara, his wife and cousin. This lineage is now chanted in many Zen centers in the United States. At the same time, there remains opposition to chanting the lineage of women. There are those who still prefer only to chant the male lineage, which starts with Bibashi Buddha, one of the seven buddhas to Shakyamuni Buddha, and moves onward through a list of legendary and historical individuals stretching up to the present.

In my view, when the term *ancestor* is used instead of *patriarch*, it broadens the lineage to include ancestors of all genders and deepens the significance of offerings being made in ceremony. The use of *ancestor* as opposed to *patriarch* also broadens our conception of who is a holder of Buddha's wisdom and who acts on behalf of everyone while making offerings to ancestors. Being inclusive of all ancestors is one way of utilizing Zen practice to eliminate oppression among us.

There is a field of all awakened ones, on every continent. We are making offerings to the awakened ancestors of all living beings. It is a ceremonial gesture to enact wellness and liberation for all—not only Buddhists or for those in the closed quarters of Buddhist monasteries and centers.

Often when I speak of ancestors in Zen Buddhist communities, folks think of the indigenous cultures of other continents. They think *jungle, primitive, primal*. They may think, "No, not us. That's not what we do here in Buddhism." This rejection causes an immediate severance from ancient practices, practices that are at least eight thousand to ten thousand years older than Buddhism and are the roots of Buddhism. When I notice such intentional turning away from the notion of ancestors—when someone says they don't understand this "ancestors stuff"—I always point out the making of offerings to the great ancestor Buddha.

Shakyamuni Buddha is an ancestor to whom we make daily physical offerings in Zen. While we are not worshipping Buddha, we are acknowledging the teachings that came through him. And, moving to the transpersonal sense, we make offerings to the lineage of Buddha across all genders and in all places and times.

For the sake of our shamanic exploration of Zen, let's stick with the historical Buddha for a moment, as there are aspects of his life story that deserve a deeper look. Ancestor Shakyamuni Buddha was described in early Buddhist literature as having magical powers. Those powers were often what drew people to him. In the modern world, with its preference for rational and secular explanations, the presence and celebration of these powers in the sutras has often been seen as embarrassing and written off as unnecessary cultural trappings. Fortunately, there are some texts left that provide evidence of Buddha as shaman and seer.

Sam van Schaik quotes another Buddhist studies scholar, Bryan Cuevas, on this issue. Cuevas states that some of the earliest Buddhist sutras from the Pali canon portray the Buddha as having wonder-working powers, including the capacity for paranormal activities such as multiplication of the body, the ability to appear and disappear at will, and the capacity to walk on water.[1] It is well-known that upon his enlightenment, Buddha was reputed to have gained a kind of omniscience, including the ability to see his own past lives as well as those of others he met. And supernormal powers were not considered to be something only a full Buddha could obtain. Bradley S. Clough, another Buddhist scholar, shares what is called the Five Higher Knowledges or *abhinnas*, which are integral in South Asian Buddhism. "The overall acceptance of the idea of attainment of certain extraordinary psychic powers by those adepts who have reached advanced stages of meditation is one of the most ancient and consistent features of South Asian Buddhism, from early Pali texts to treatises of the latter phases of the Mahayana in this region," he writes.[2] Clough translates the Five Higher Knowledges as:

1. knowledge of the varieties of supernormal power
2. divine ear element
3. knowledge comprehending the mind or cognizing others' thoughts
4. knowledge of recollection of past lives
5. divine eye, or knowledge of passing away and rebirth[3]

As far back as you can go in Buddhist literature, spells and magical powers are there. For instance, van Schaik has noted that discussion of magical powers is present in Buddhist texts found in Afghanistan that are among the earliest on record. Thus, it is possible to acknowledge Shakyamuni Buddha not only as an ancestor but also as a shamanic ancestor. My sense is that Buddha went on a vision quest when he left the palace to meditate on the suffering of human beings. He was joined by others who considered sitting upon the earth as a way to see the nature of this life—of birth, illness, old age, and death. The Buddha set out to face the issues of life that concerned him. His quest led to a deep seeing and knowing about suffering. After fasting for days, if not months, dwindling down to the bone, it was clear that the impermanence of life could be a dilemma of birth or a reckoning with death. He came to realize that he didn't exist without his family and those of the Shakya tribe. He understood clearly, as is apparent in his teachings, that we possess nothing, not even our lives. In living, we make a mark in the world, and from that action, a certain consequence will occur sometime in the future, perhaps a future we will not live to see.

Many Zen practitioners and teachers do not see Buddha as a shaman, but I encourage us to look closely at some of the elements in the story of his awakening. The Buddha is said to have lived on one grain of rice per day during his ascetic period; to have sat in the elements, barely clothed for days; and to have returned as a teacher filled with timeless teachings that he gathered from lucid dreams. Reflecting on this story, I see the Buddha as a dreamer who taught not from his intellect but from the wisdom of his quest, as would any practitioner of the earth. We can look at those stories as myths or exaggerations and dismiss their meanings; we can take them as culturally relative stories crafted according to the expectations of listeners from that time. But I think it is worthwhile to look at the implications of the stories when taken literally.

I suspect that Buddha was taught by shamans, perhaps religious seers who visited his home when he was a prince. Perhaps he was taught by other shamanic practitioners how to survive on a grain of rice, to go without water, and to live in the woods, naked or nearly naked to the elements. In Buddha's attempt to understand the world from which he had been separated and protected, he chose magic and shamanism—the path that was available in ancient times, long before religion or science.

∘ ∘ ∘

I feel, however, that the real magic is not in honoring the historical Buddha as a shamanic ancestor, though that is an important step. It is in the practice of experiencing Buddha as a reflection of our own magical or enlightened nature. In making offerings to Buddha, one is making offerings to one's own buddha nature, to one's own capacity to awaken. In Zen, it is said, "If you see the Buddha, kill him." This points to a final liberation, the emptying of substance from what we think of as real—even sacred concepts like "Buddha." Another popular teaching is, "A painted rice cake does not satisfy hunger," which is to say everything is a painting, including Buddha—the reality even of Buddha is constructed.

The statue of Buddha is a mirror image of our own essential lives, and I believe this is the reason so many people, whether Buddhist or not, include a statue of Buddha in their homes. Seeing an image of the Buddha is a way of accessing the silence and stillness that is innately within us. Likewise, when we see the rituals involved in honoring Buddha, we see ourselves, and this creates a diverse imagery of Buddha, with different ways to access what we need for our particular lives. So, when making offerings, we are doing such to a diverse buddha nature.

Paula Arai, a scholar of Buddhism, has studied how nuns in a Soto Zen monastery in Japan empowered their buddha nature based on the imagery of their culture. She witnessed two rituals the women used to direct energy toward what they felt important in their lives. One ritual, the *Anan Koshiki*, was a way to address the need for "social change through nonconfrontational methods." The other, the *Jizo Nagashi* ritual, highlighted how "an ancestral memorial rite . . . functions as part of a larger healing process." Arai writes, "Together, the rituals indicated the creative ways in which Sōtō Zen Buddhist women incorporate ritual into their lives and, in turn, how rituals are an actualization of their concerns."[4] In both rituals, there was an awareness of Buddha, of buddha nature, and of the healing and transformative aspects of ritual. Most important, the rituals are not necessarily about worshipping Buddha as a figure but about utilizing Buddha's seeing and awakening as their own. Seeing Buddha, they see themselves.

There is a beautiful song in the African Malawi culture that represents seeing a diverse buddha nature in each other and honoring each other. It is sung while facing another person. You sing to the person that you see them—"I see you," and in turn, they do the same. When one person acknowledges that they see the other, it is a ritual of mirroring, of empowering. And it supports awakening to the reality that there isn't only *my* life but also that there is life. There is valuing life. We honor that life in ritual and ceremony when we make offerings.

∴

When we make offerings to the ancestors of our lives—be it the bloodline of our relatives or the lineage of our spiritual community, or be it offerings to animals, trees, plants, moon, or sun—we are making a mark in the world. When we offer ourselves, our lives, to a practice of awakening, we are making a mark of awakening for all. It is important when you stand before an altar giving offerings that you are aware of what mark you are making.

During my training as *shuso* (head student) at San Francisco Zen Center, my teacher, Zenkei Blanche Hartman (1926–2016), was showing me how to offer incense in the

Buddha Hall. The next week, I would be offering incense for the first time as part of the ritual of my first shuso talk. I closely watched Zenkei as she walked up to the Buddha statue and held the incense up toward Buddha. Next, her lips began to move, but I could not hear the words. What was she saying? Later, she informed me that there is a chant one says when offering incense, but that the chant had gotten lost in the development of the temple over the years. At that moment, I was certain that there was more that had gotten lost in the cracks that occur in transitions between teachers. What rituals that Suzuki Roshi taught had been abandoned over the years? In recognizing such loss in the moment, I asked her to repeat the chant out loud. I desperately tried to remember it so that it could be written down and preserved. I promptly forgot but later asked her to say the chant again and again.

INCENSE-OFFERING VERSE AT THE ALTAR

SILA KO (precept incense)
SAMADHI KO (samadhi incense)
MUKATA KO (liberation incense)
Illuminating the clouds of the Dharma realm
Serving innumerable Buddhas in the ten directions,
Perfuming the seeing of the tranquil world.

Although, nowadays, flowers at San Francisco Zen Center are offered instead of incense due to people's health issues, the chant is still a gem. Zenkei Roshi practiced in the Suzuki Roshi lineage for forty-five years. During her years as an ordained Zen Buddhist nun (as she liked to be called, not "priest"), she dropped many gems into the pockets of others. The chanting gem she gave me that day was held with reverence, as it brought boundlessness to the moment. Suddenly, I was not worried about any judgment about how I offered incense. Making the offering wasn't about me at all. It was about the ritual, the mark that needed to be made for everyone and for those who would lead such a ritual in the future. Instead of fear, learning the lost verse brought curiosity and a deeper thirst for the things lost along the way in transmitting Zen practice.

Prolonged Rituals
of Seeing
and Listening

On the fourth day of silence, the world outside the walls no longer exists. I am speechless. And it is not because there are no words on my tongue. There is a forest with ninety people surrounding me— animals in the wilderness. Their voices are no longer, but there is a grunt or two. Some wander the forest, stomping. Some move quietly. Some are flying. The cloth of our robes rustles. Chanting is soothing when the mind goes places in the dark silence. And then I come upon this place as if lounging on a bouncing branch. I know that if I come into my mind, I will become afraid that the branch will snap. In the meantime, I am a bird.

I only share with particular people the things I have seen of other worlds while on shamanic journeys. One reason is because many people in this country do not believe in visions, altered states, or extrasensory perception such as clairvoyance. Beginning very early in the colonial era, there have been violent efforts, including the annihilation of African and Native American medicine people and the burning of those accused as witches, to suppress that which was viewed as magic. This is the case even though, prior to the Enlightenment era, those who opposed what they saw as devil's magic were largely believers and supporters of Christian ideas and practices that most people today would also view as magic. Such demonization of the magic of other cultures has had staying power: still today, many activities of indigenous religions, especially African religions such as Vodou, are deemed "devil's work" and rendered inferior. Such demonization of what isn't Christian has a long history. For this reason, some teachers from Asia and early Western practitioners of Buddhism were cautious about presenting or engaging with a religion that seemed counter to the dominant Christianity, and their fears played a large role in the modernization of Buddhism. What is more, since the Enlightenment era, the anti-magic stance has evolved to include strong strains of suspicion toward *anything* that doesn't conform to supposedly scientific, rationalist standards. There is much effort in contemporary times to scientifically show the value and worth of meditation perhaps to those who are skeptical of what many call the spirit, unseen world, Buddhism, and spirituality in general.

Fortunately, I have a number of friends who are open to the vastness of the heart, mind, and consciousness and embrace the experience of seeing beyond this world. We love the wondrousness of what is revealed in the unseen. Some of these friends are Zen priests who rarely speak of their experiences to others. Is it still taboo today within Zen communities to reveal a mystical side of their Zen experience?

The suppression of magic or otherworldly activities takes place in many religions. It even occurs in indigenous spiritual traditions where alignment with the dominant culture is critical to survival. Because we are human beings, I am certain that Zen has not gone untouched by this suppression. In fact, before the historical Shakyamuni Buddha, what we call meditation (secular or religious) was simply called "trance." In the shamanic world, a trance is a self-induced state of consciousness that is accessed as a way to see how to serve one's community through healing, dealing with injustices, or guiding the living and the dead. The act of trance by shamans is completely selfless. If we were to understand the lineage from trance to meditation, we would better understand the nature of Zen.

I have felt like a buffalo in medicine ceremonies. I have flown with an eagle feather while dancing in the wind of a Lakota arbor. And I have felt like a tiny bird bouncing on a branch during zazen. I have had many glimpses of being and not being while sitting. The lights have been dimmed. The chants chanted. The incense offered. And then there is this feeling that I could very well be touching the moon, the one in the dewdrop. I am clear that I have experienced meditation as a shamanic journey, particularly zazen, where there is no one guiding the breath, not even the practitioner.

* *

Zazen is the core of Zen practice. *Za* means "sitting" and *Zen* means "meditation." The word *Zen* has come to have many meanings in various contexts, but in the context of this book, it is the practice of seated meditation without being guided. There is no goal in mind or effort to improve one's personality. Shunryu Suzuki Roshi said, "Zazen practice is the direct experience of our true nature."[1] Dainin Katagiri Roshi said, "Zazen is the right gate for entering the Buddha-dharma. But the Buddha-dharma is actually human life."[2] In the view of these renowned Zen teachers, the conventional thinking in regard to Zen and zazen is far beyond what anyone can imagine.

Zazen is different than secular meditation, which generally means using meditation as a calming technique or method to remain present in the moment. As with zazen, secular meditation often uses the breath as a focal point, but there generally is no transformation of how one perceives the world or their life. Usually, there is an intention to leave religious teachings out of secular meditation. There is no seeking God, as in some religious traditions, or discovering the nature of life, as in Zen meditation. Zazen is not meant to calm one's nerves, although that may be a result of the awareness zazen can bring over time. It is more than a religious activity as it might appear. It is more than a practice even though many call it that. Zazen is a *prolonged* ritual of seeing and listening. It is a shamanic process and a way of life.

Eventually, in zazen, you become the meditation as it arises in you with each breath. It is no longer something you do or something on the to-do list. Since zazen can potentially transform you at the core of your life, it is meant for the rare individual who is willing to enter meditation as ritual, deepening the understanding of life and death. Zazen is more aligned with the ancient meditations of indigenous medicine people of where those in training leave to sit still upon the earth in silence over an extended period of time. They take many trips to the mountains, so to speak. Similarly, zazen is a slow walk in the wilderness. Step by step, bell after bell, chant after chant, breath after breath over many years—and without effort, one may reach a vast field of illumination.

To take one's seat in zazen is to sit upon the earth. It is to connect to the source of our lives, which is the breath passed on by ancestors. In Zen, bowing to one's seat before sitting is to bow to that source, to ancestors. Likewise, before sitting down, bowing into the space of the temple, which is to acknowledge the sacred space where we are held in our journey with the breath. To bow to a statue of Buddha is to revere an enlightened life. It is often emphasized in Zen to adopt an upright yet relaxed sitting posture. But there is no need for good posture in the seat of zazen if there is no understanding of the purpose of the posture in relationship to seeing, to listening, to awakening.

Unlike secular meditation, zazen has been passed down through many generations via distinct instructions on how to sit. Most commonly, in Japan and now in the United States, these instructions have been conveyed by Dogen Zenji's *Fukanzazengi* (Universally Recommended Instructions for Zazen). In this view of many sitting generations, it is not you who is sitting alone, without a lineage of those who came before you. Zazen is done for the sake of humanity now and in the future. We may enter meditation as a psychological endeavor or an act of social justice and wellness, but this intergenerational lineage view holds out the possibility of a spiritual collective transformation through the collective ritual of zazen and ceremony. Thank goodness, zazen goes on after we die, constantly being transmitted from one breath to another, sustaining eons of wisdom. Zazen is neverending.

Most Buddhists throughout history have not relied on an extensive sitting practice, instead using study and chanting/singing to open doors of the mind and heart. Chanting, which I will return to later in the book, can provide an environment that encourages awakening through the words that encompass the teachings. But in the Zen tradition, sitting practice is given special emphasis. In zazen, awakening comes through the body in sitting still and breathing. We often feel we are breathing until we sit down and realize we are barely breathing. The breath connects the body and mind. This is the reason why, when we breathe, we might feel ourselves relax; the mind is on the breath, the body, and not everything external to you. This kind of slow, steady breathing can facilitate being aware of how the body moves.

Zazen also incorporates kinhin, or walking meditation, as ritual. This ritual is the slow walk of zazen. The movement is meant to sync with the breath, honed in sitting meditation and with touching the ground with the toe and heel. The power of this way of walking is often missed in contemporary Zen centers, where the participants tend to leave the ritual of zazen, mentally and physically, at kinhin for various reasons. What is missed, then, is the experience of moving with the state of consciousness that comes from sitting. This meditation in movement deepens zazen as the participants in the ritual circumambulate in various patterns in the zendo. There is an awareness of the body in how it walks and breathes, and an awareness of how pain resides in the body and mind and how it relates to the simple action of walking. Kinhin is an experience of how movement and action connect to the mind and thus create suffering and/or awakening.

From awakened ones in all indigenous cultures throughout space and time and from ancient sages of all genders and ethnicities, the teachings of awakening have been brought forth through stillness. As mentioned earlier, meditation is the most ancient and enduring path toward wisdom, vision, or insight. If we release meditation from its confines in various religions, we begin to see the expansive use of this earth-based way of understanding life and navigating the unknown.

Many of us hope to understand life before living it. Coming to meditation, we want to protect ourselves with the practice, so we learn to breathe as part of our effort to not make mistakes or cause more suffering in our lives. We try to see the potholes before we stumble; perhaps we even think we can prevent the possible tragedies of life. With this approach, everything desired from meditation lies in the future: "If I meditate, in the future, I will be calm." "I will no longer have high blood pressure." "I will be able to handle racism better." It makes sense that the challenges of our daily lives become the center of our quest during meditation. We can use the difficulties of life to awaken, but not without a way to see into those difficulties.

Usually, pain, some kind of disruption, or loss in life is what leads people to the path of meditation. In my first sitting experience, everything hurt. It was difficult to find a position to sit in. Every pain or experience of suffering in my life marched forward in my mind and body, causing more pain than had the actual experiences. Herein lies the danger of just sitting without guidance. It's like packing your bags and going off into the woods for a shamanic journey without so much as a clue to what you're doing. You have thoughts about what you're doing, but you have not been prepared or given guidance for the journey. You carry an empty medicine bag.

Before taking a seat on the earth, shamans prepare themselves with prayer and guidance from those who have gone before them. They prepare their bodies for the journey. They fill their medicine bag with teachings and experiences that have led to awakening.

Upon starting my walk onto the path of Zen, my body had not been prepared for the enduring test of stillness. I was unaware of how to warm my body before sitting. I did not know to use the stretches, movement, or yoga that I had learned earlier in my life to slow the heart rate and induce stillness. The zazen instruction I received was about posture, with little guidance on how to attend to the suffering that arises. As a new person, I was not ready to choose a teacher and needed guidance on how to do such. I found myself relying on the sense of being in an endurance challenge—a feeling I had used to survive before coming to Zen. Then it completely broke apart during a three-week intensive. I often talk about this critical time because the emotional, physical, and spiritual breakdown was the beginning of my Zen practice. I saw my pain break open. I could no longer hold the old things I had learned. I could not explain to anyone outside of Zen what I was doing with my life. I was in the wilderness with few skills. It was time to choose someone to walk with me. Who would show me the way of a shaman in the woods? Until I was ready to choose a teacher, I found some skills with Grandmother Mind, loving yet strict, to help me walk this uneven new path.

It is difficult to find a spiritual guide in our modern day, as we live so far away from the earth. The ancient way of being enlightened feels as though it is buried with the ancestors. We have moved away from nature—the shaman's only source of wisdom and healing. We are no longer hunters and gatherers, so it is hard to find someone with the ancient skills of awakening. It takes time and a readiness for such guidance to come to you. Wisdom and skills may not come through a person at all but through the earth itself, as it did for Shakyamuni Buddha.

Fortunately, what is ancient remains in our bones. Although I have had many teachers, Buddhist and non-Buddhist, I spend time out in the wilderness to access the wisdom of the bones. I came to Zen with some knowing from long Sundays at church in my youth, from African and Native American ceremony, and from my Nichiren Buddhist practice, but I still needed help with the strange and silent way of Zen.

There is a huge blazing fire at the door of Zen, as in every transformative practice. It can be turned away from or entered into. It will burn all you think you know of yourself to ashes. This can be frightening since we enter, having gone thirsty for peace, looking for water.

THE PORTAL OF ZAZEN

Meditation is now sought by many for various reasons. However, Zen is for the rare person who is not only looking to attend to suffering but also desires to immerse into the waters of our universal experience of birth and death. It is for those who ask the question, "What is this life?" but do not really want an answer. Zazen is for those who are willing to sit with the medicine and wonder what effects it will have on their spiritual illnesses. What will be seen in the dark? Who will come to speak loudly in the silence? Zen is for those who thrive on the intangible, the ambiguous, the amorphous, and the infinite. We are stars forever suspended in nowhere. This is what makes Zen appear difficult and strange to many. You really can't see Zen. You can only experience it after some time of walking the path.

In zazen, it is only through the body that awakening is revealed. Being embodied, we bring our hardships with us. But we don't contemplate them. If we contemplate on the hardships, we are caught in our minds, spending time analyzing our lives. In these situations, we might further the hardships. The shamans I have experienced have great challenges in daily life, but when doing the work of transformation, they set the things of the world aside for the expansion needed to see through the suffering. In both Zen and shamanism, we are led *through* (not around) the difficulties of our embodiment. The oneness of embodiment and boundlessness is experienced together. In my own experience, the life I have lived in the midst of oppression gives me soil to grow *through and into* awakening.

We can see the oneness of embodiment and boundlessness through Zen art practices. The Zen author, artist, and scholar Stephen Addiss defines *Zenga* (Zen art) as "the brushwork of leading Zen monks or occasionally of other monks and laymen who have studied Zen deeply enough to be imbued with its spirit."[3] Most analysis of this calligraphic embodiment of Zen energy has focused on its sense of suddenness and transcendence. But another scholar, Charlotte Eubanks, argues that many examples of Zen calligraphy convey other qualities such as balance and calm.[4] The art of Zen, especially Zen calligraphy, is in fact the spirit of the embodiment of zazen. This spirit of zazen is also expressed in Obaku Zen (a sect in Japan), where monks practice what is called spirit writing, in which they write from the voices of the spirits of ancient ancestors.

In Zen, zazen becomes the portal through which we attend to our disconnection and disappointments with life and perhaps find reconnection and transformation in the breath. This breath can be expressed through the art of Zen or through any activity of our lives. In essence, when entering the portal of zazen, the expression of life is not through ego, thoughts, emotions, or expectations. With calligraphy, the brush becomes one with the body in expressing life as breathed in zazen. Then, there is no conscious effort in creating art or life. In the portal of zazen, there is unbounded life energy and the possibility of bringing forth the spirit of life rather than our idea of reality. Of course, this experience I speak of here takes time and guidance.

. . .

Zazen is central to experiencing the awakened consciousness that existed prior to us taking a seat in the wild. Like Buddha, we sit on the earth and allow the seeds of awakening to sprout in our lives. A seeing practice, such as zazen, is the only method to gather such seeds and plant them in every activity of our lives.

Zazen begins and continues with sitting, but over time, we come to find it is not confined to sitting. Everything in Zen practice is done through the state of consciousness brought by zazen. In rituals and ceremonies, there is zazen. This is an altered consciousness, in the sense that anything that takes your mind and heart from the chaos of the world and centers it on the breath and the earth is an altered consciousness—a transformed heart and mind. Granted, the depth of the altered consciousness is not consistent from one person to the next, but neither are shamans equal in the height and expression of their ascended consciousness.

It is easy to speak of being in zazen amid everyday activity. But do you know how it feels to come awake in zazen? Have you had an awakening while doing the laundry? Could it be that you are practicing mindfulness rather than zazen? Although mindfulness can be a gateway to zazen, the difference, in my experience, is that zazen is a shamanic practice where there is no checking in with the mind. The mind is given an open field in which to see the entire universe, or that which could never be imagined.

If we are in zazen, then we have given ourselves over to the silence. We are not seeking awakening as much as we are seeing our lives or life in general. While in the wilderness of zazen, we are the shamans of our lives, listening and awakening to nature in order to understand and live consciously within our innate relationship with the world around us. We have some knowledge of life, and at the same time, we don't know what wisdom is to be discovered. In ancient times (and in some Japanese Buddhist traditions), a relationship with deities and spirits was sought as a way to access wisdom we lacked. Some of us modern Zen practitioners dare say we have heard or speak to deities and spirits. In zazen, some have reported having a vision, an appearance of spirit or *makyo* as it is called in Medieval Japanese. But in Soto Zen, we are taught to not make a fuss about it, not to be fascinated with ourselves, and so we don't readily share such experiences. Some will say that altered states of consciousness have nothing to do with the realm of zazen. But how can we go through the portal of zazen and never hear the cries of the earth? Do we not dream as Buddha did? Do not the spirits of nature affect our lives? These exploratory questions deepened my curiosity about seeing Zen meditation as shamanic journeying.

Of course, I am not the first to explore the intersection

of Buddhism and shamanism. In her essay "The Journey: Buddhism and Shamanism at the Crossroads," Isa Gucciardi, a teacher and practitioner of Shamanism writes:

> Meditation and the shamanic journey are processes that take place in the altered state. The altered state helps seekers connect with their inner experience in a broader way. We spend most of our time in the vigilant, problem-solving state of consciousness of the conscious mind. In Buddhism, the goal of working with the altered state is similar to the goal of working with the altered state in shamanism—to move beyond the confines of the conscious mind and thereby receive information or insight that cannot be accessed in working with the conscious mind alone.[5]

Our conscious mind has limitations. When we make efforts to transform our suffering, we become aware of these limitations. For this reason, we might find ourselves entering a path of meditation to deal with pain and suffering, including physical and spiritual illness. A practitioner of Zen, like the shaman, is devoted to attending to illnesses, and in turn, the healing affects the collective family, community, and so forth. Both shamanism and Buddhism work at the root of illness by shifting awareness inward to access other states of consciousness. Accessing these states without effort is where Buddhist and shamanic traditions meet.

Zazen shares certain elements of shamanism: self-realization, enhanced dreams, heightened intuition, deep concentration, a strengthened relationship with the wisdom of nature, reflection, speaking to ancestors in ceremony, and living a life of spiritual inquiry into the unseen. In Zen and shamanism, you put aside conceptualization and intellectual understanding to return to a vast state of consciousness, the open field of your life. Zen has its own names for these kinds of experiences.

EXPERIENCES OF AWAKENING IN THE ALTERED CONSCIOUSNESS OF ZAZEN

The Zen tradition teaches that altered states of consciousness are not the goal, and zazen is not a means to an end. Yet many Zen meditators experience altered states in zazen. This is one of the paradoxes of Zen: we meditate without the notion of a quest for awakening, yet there are various levels of awakening that can be experienced in zazen. These are mostly talked about in traditions other than Soto Zen. You will hear more about states of consciousness within zazen in Zen traditions such as Rinzai, Obaku, or Sanbo Kyodan. You might hear of the quest for satori or kensho—Japanese Zen terms for awakening experiences characterized by sudden direct perception. You might read about samadhi, meditative absorption. You may also know of koan (kufu) practice, where a Zen master or teacher uses a riddle or puzzle to expand the consciousness of a student in order to deepen insight.

I suspect that there are many undocumented experiences within zazen, and meditation more broadly, of increased ability to see the unseen, heightened intuition, and magnified lucid dreaming. In my own case, as noted above, it was the latter that led to my developing a sense of connection with the ancestors and produced the Black Angel oracle that came to me while sleeping. Although shamanic experiences in Zen may often go undocumented, many such experiences, being described in the traditional language of Zen, may therefore appear as non-shamanic. For this reason, I would like to explore some of the most common Zen terms for awakening experiences and consider them from a shamanic perspective.

A simple meaning of *satori* is to attain self-realization from the practice of zazen. Philip Kapleau, a pioneer in bringing Zen to the West, gave breakthrough teachings on practicing zazen without a Zen master and reaching satori in his classic book *The Three Pillars of Zen*. There are accounts therein of ordinary lay people reaching satori, which Kapleau describes as "the actualization or unfoldment of the inherently enlightened Bodhi-mind with which all are endowed."[6] Satori can also be described as the sudden and direct perception of the true nature of mind or enlightenment.

Kensho, which is often interchanged with satori, carries the element of spontaneity. As an experience of awakening, it is described in similar terms to the universe's coming into being in "the big bang"—a sudden and powerful event that changes everything and from which there is no going back. So, kensho can go beyond perception and create something new and unimagined. Kensho is a term more commonly used in Rinzai Zen, whereas Soto Zen tends to focus more on satori. Satori is a deep spiritual experience that includes the immediate and sudden perception of kensho but is experienced as an unfolding in which one tries to discern what has been seen. It is not that there is something suddenly seen with the eyes, like what might happen in a shamanic journey, or that the experience has made you more profound than another.

Both satori and kensho involve a direct realization of life, akin to a shamanic experience. These are the kinds of experiences that cannot be obtained through a teacher or a book. It is not what some refer to as an "ah-ha" moment, an epiphany. Instead, as Meido Moore Roshi, Zen and martial arts teacher, writes in his book *Hidden Zen: Practices for Sudden Awakening and Embodied Realization*, "Seeing one's nature—kensho—... simply refers to the moment that one discovers or knows something for oneself, directly and experientially, rather than through the descriptions of others."[7] Dogen Zenji, the founder of Soto Zen, called kensho a dropping away of body and mind. D. T. Suzuki (Suzuki Daisetsu, 1870–1966), in *An Introduction to Zen Buddhism*, said of kensho:

> When the mind has been so trained as to be able to realize a state of perfect void in which there is not a trace of consciousness left, even the sense of being unconscious having departed; in other words, when all forms of mental activity are swept away clean from the field of consciousness, leaving the mind like the sky devoid of every speck of cloud, a mere broad expense of blue, Dhyana [meditation] is said to have reached its perfection.[8]

Shamanic experience is not only to see the unseen—for instance, the spirit of a tree, a flower, a bird, or a person—but to recognize it. You may sit before a shaman and wait for them to see you—not the you in front of them, but the you who exists in the unseen realm. The shaman, in recognizing the spirit, can then guide you away from suffering and toward wellness. When Buddha raised the udumbara flower, a tiny white tulip on a thin thread stem, Mahakasyapa, a disciple, saw the spirit of the gesture, of the flower. In that moment, he saw the Buddha's spirit as enlightenment. He recognized enlightenment without being told it was such. While there is a debate as to whether the udumbara flower is mythical, it depicts a kensho experience between the Buddha and a disciple. Mahakasyapa's shamanic moment is a story of kensho that holds great significance in the Zen tradition.

In contrast to Rinzai Zen, Soto Zen avoids the idea of a *quest* for kensho, preferring to emphasize no-gaining mind or just sitting. Although this approach is intentional and has its benefits, it can result in practitioners who experience kensho denying the experience of a flash or glimpse of what's behind the curtain of life. In zazen, whether we experience kensho or satori, we are guided toward our own curtains. Zazen pulls the curtain back and reveals life.

Does Soto Zen inherently include kensho as an aspiration without working toward it? Moore, a Rinzai Zen teacher, writes, "The truth is that nothing the mind may conceive, project, or visualize is the wisdom of kensho. Rather, kensho is to arrive at a seeing—an intimate and wordless knowing—of the nature of *that which sees and knows.*"[9] Kensho or satori remains part of the nothingness Soto Zen teaches. In its shamanic way, zazen is not a technique for achieving in the world. It is a gateway to liberation without seeing it as such.

In essence, through zazen, we are discovering life. When we perceive it beyond our past conceptualizations, we are in direct perception with what time and space are presenting. This experience can be sudden or spontaneous, which is then considered an experience of satori and/or kensho. Once such a perception is made, repeatedly seeing in such a way enhances the depth of the seeing practice. A more dynamic zazen is possible but cannot be offered as a guarantee of practice. When we engage in zazen when there is kensho or satori, there is the possibility of a true awareness that we are interrelated to all perceived phenomena. There is no further question about what is no-self once there has been a direct and sudden experience of interrelatedness. With sudden realization, one recognizes and confirms for oneself the suchness of life. We recognize ourselves, not based on what our family, community, or culture imposes, but based on what we see of life in zazen.

Many zazen experiences enter into the realm of shamanism in the sense of awakening, though in the modern West, they typically do not come with the ability to communicate to deities or spirits. Communicating with ancestors as shamans do is for the purpose of delivering messages to the community. In that sense, accessing the altered state is not for oneself alone but for the community. If we consider zazen to be a practice in the realm of shamanism, it might assist Zen practitioners in seeing that we sit not only for ourselves but also for the well-being of others. This way of utilizing meditation is closer to the communal nature of indigenous people. For a person like myself with parents from rural Louisiana, the enhancement of one person was for the benefit of all. In this sense, selflessness is the embodiment of interbeing. Omori Sogen Roshi (1904–1994) of Chozen-ji in Hawaii, referencing a famous teaching from Dogen, said, "The entire universe is the true human body."

Zen master Kodo Sawaki (1880–1965) said, "Zazen is good for nothing." It is a famous quote of which I understood nothing until after my first *sesshin* (a traditional seven-day Zen sitting retreat). If you are waiting for something to happen in zazen, then you are looking for the results of the practice. You want something out of it for the time and money spent. If you go to a shaman, you may look for an immediate result of their work with your illnesses. But just as there are no guarantees of results in zazen, there are no guarantees of results from a shaman's assistance because there are so many other things of the body and mind, history, culture, and more affecting the experience. In the meantime, zazen and shamanic assistance give you space and time to discover life in a way that the busy world does not allow. Coming to take a seat in the zendo or at the shaman's feet is in itself the beginning and end of liberation.

The idea of just sitting without gaining is the core teaching of Zen master Dogen Zenji, the thirteenth-century founder of the Soto Zen school in Japan (an extension of the Caodong school in China). It is called *shikan-taza*, and I discuss it further below. First, however, I will briefly introduce various kinds of Zen meditation other than zazen. These earlier forms of Zen as meditation clearly have shamanic elements. I thought it would be interesting to include them to see how non-Buddhist Zen evolved toward Zen Buddhist zazen through various transmissions by the Japanese Zen masters. The source of the information is from *The Three Pillars of Zen* by Philip Kapleau.[10]

KINDS OF ZEN MEDITATION

Bompu: A nonreligious and non-philosophical Zen meditation, Bompu Zen can be done by anybody. The goal of Bompu Zen is to improve physical and mental health, eliminate psychosomatic sickness, and improve health in general. It is also meant to help concentration and control of the mind. Bompu is different than the popular zazen of Soto Zen in that it isn't meant to resolve the questions of human existence and one's relation to the universe.

Gedo: A kind of Zen meditation that is practiced to cultivate supranormal powers and skills beyond the reach of the ordinary person. Gedo enables magical acts such as staring at a sparrow so they become paralyzed or becoming able to walk barefoot on sharp sword blades. These feats of Gedo Zen occur through cultivation of *joriki*, which Kapleau defines as "the particular strength or power which comes with the strenuous practice of mind concentration."[11] Aiming for the cultivation of joriki is a kind of Zen that is not Buddhist. Another object of Gedo is rebirth in various heavens, which likewise places the practice adjacent to but clearly outside of Buddhist Zen. Zen Buddhists do not crave rebirth.

Shojo: The word *shojo* means "small vehicle." Shojo Zen meditation takes you from delusion to enlightenment—clearly a Zen Buddhist goal—but it does so only for the individual. This is unlike Mahayana Buddhism (including Zen), where one's practices are also for the benefit of all. Despite this non-Mahayana orientation, Shojo Zen is still considered Zen Buddhism.

Daijo: Meaning "the great vehicle," Daijo is the teaching of Mahayana Zen. Here, we are moving closer to a kind of zazen of just sitting, shikan-taza. It differs from shikan-taza though in that it has a central purpose of kensho, seeing into your essential nature and realizing the Way in your daily life. In Daijo Zen, you break through an illusory view of the universe and experience absolute, undifferentiated reality. A Zen meditation practice that ignores satori-awakening, enlightenment, is not Daijo. Daijo zazen is awakening to your true nature, but upon enlightenment, you realize that zazen is more than a means to enlightenment. Within Daijo, one can mistake zazen as a means.

Saijojo/Shikan-taza: This zazen was practiced by all the Buddhas of the past, including Shakyamuni Buddha and Amida Buddha. Saijojo is the expression of absolute life. Dogen Zenji is known to be the premier teacher of this form of zazen—the zazen of cultivating the empty field. It is called *shikan-taza*. Shikan-taza is zazen without inquiry, counting, or following the breaths. It is not a busy meditation.

Zazen as Ritual

In Soto Zen, we align with Dogen and practice just sitting as our form of meditation. But this does not mean that Zen meditation has not been influenced by other or earlier forms of zazen such as those listed above that include shamanic aspects.

Taigen Leighton, a contemporary Zen teacher, author, and scholar, has made a similar point. He describes shikan-taza as an "objectless meditation." But he also states that it includes in its background "intent focus on a particular object. Such objects traditionally have included colored disks, candle flames, various aspects of breath, incantations, ambient sound, physical sensations or postures, spiritual figures, mandalas including geometric arrangements of such figures or of symbols representing them, and teaching stories or key phrases from such stories."[12]

I would add that the shamanic-like awakening of kensho or satori is not necessarily invisible in shikan-taza because it is considered an objectless form of meditation. There just is no *working toward* kensho or satori. The awareness from just sitting lays a foundation for some to experience effortless or spontaneous awakening, as one would in shamanic journey. However, this experience is rare among practitioners today.

Zazen in Soto Zen is a ceremonial, ritual expression of awakened awareness. When I read about this view in Taigen Leighton's essay "Zazen as an Enactment Ritual," it resonated with my own experience of taking my seat in the zendo.[13] Although it may have been pain that led me to that seat, the practice is not a reaction to the pain but the simple embodying, in ritual, of the awareness of my entire life. Through the extensive preparation and ritualized meditation of zazen, I found an ease with steadying myself for what would be revealed.

A further support for seeing zazen as an enactment ritual comes straight from its associations with the Vajrayana or tantric branch of Buddhism. As I mentioned earlier, there once existed an ancient Tibetan Zen that was influenced by the tantric tradition. Furthermore, Leighton notes that Japanese tantric or esoteric (*mikkyo*) heritage was a part of all medieval Japanese Buddhism and is present in all forms of Japanese Zen, including the Soto Zen of the West.[14] In addition, I discovered, thanks to Leighton, that Dogen and Nichiren, the founding teachers of my chosen paths, studied Japanese Vajrayana and therefore their teachings were influenced by shamanism. The discovery of zazen as a tantric ritual sealed my suspicions of the hidden shamanic bones of Zen.

To see zazen as an enactment ritual of tantric nature, you need simply look at Dogen's teaching called the *Fukanzazengi*. As mentioned earlier, this is his famous rendition of a teaching from Chinese Ch'an, where the ritual for zazen is laid out. Although only a few pages long, this text has exerted enormous influence on Soto Zen. Here is an excerpt (with *sanzen* initially used in place of *zazen*):

> For sanzen, a quiet room is suitable. Eat and drink moderately. Cast aside all involvements and cease all affairs. Do not think good or bad. Do not administer pros and cons. Cease all the movements of the conscious mind, the gauging of all thought and views. Have no designs on becoming a buddha. Sanzen has nothing whatever to do with sitting or lying down.
>
> At the site of your regular sitting, spread out thick matting and place a cushion above it. Sit either in the full-lotus or half-lotus position. In the full-lotus position, you first place your right foot on your left thigh and your left foot on your right thigh. In the half-lotus, you simply press your left foot against your right thigh. You should have your robes and belt loosely bound and arranged in order. Then place your right hand on your left leg and your left palm (facing

upward) on your right palm, thumb-tips touching. Thus sit upright in correct bodily posture, neither inclining to the left nor to the right, neither leaning forward nor backward. Be sure your ears are on a plane with your shoulders and your nose in line with your navel. Place your tongue against the front roof of your mouth, with teeth and lips both shut. Your eyes should always remain open, and you should breathe gently through your nose. Once you have adjusted your posture, take a deep breath, inhale and exhale, rock your body right and left and settle into a steady, immovable sitting position. Think of not-thinking. How do you think of not-thinking? Non-thinking. This in itself is the essential art of zazen.

The zazen I speak of is not learning meditation. It is simply the dharma-gate of repose and bliss, the practice-realization of totally culminated enlightenment.[15]

Dogen's *Fukanzazengi* was the teaching loved by my teacher, Zenkei Blanche Hartman. When she led ango (practice periods), she would always present this teaching. We'd chant *Fukanzazengi* in the early mornings, a little before dawn. Most students, including myself, would be half asleep, so we would mumble through this long instruction on how to sit zazen. Some might have said after chanting the instructions a hundred times, "I got it!" Few knew that chanting the instructions is itself a ritual meant to assist in connecting to awakening.

Since I mostly sat in a chair, due to physical ability, it was difficult for me to see the posture as connecting to the earth. In a chair, there was no fluffing my cushions on the tatami mats or other ritual preparations for the journey besides bowing to the seat and bowing out to the space of the zendo. If one were to view the preparation, it might be seen as rigid, overly prescriptive, or filled with pomp and circumstance. Zen practitioners might be seen as fussing with cushions and robes, when in fact there is a precise ritual for zazen in progress. If you watch closely, you will see the shaman at work creating a space where the work of awakening can occur. You can see in the instructions for the ritual after the offerings are made, the shaman taking on a particular posture in front of the ancestor Buddha, finding a center in the body to aligning oneself with the earth. All of this to avail oneself for effortless kensho.

Once, I was extremely intentional with how I came to my seat for zazen. I went slow at the annoyance of other practitioners waiting for me to do the quickest bow possible and get out of their way. I puffed up my support cushions for my back. I slowly sat down and arranged my robes in folds. After the incense was offered, I slid into the silence, all tucked in. I began weeping. Suddenly, the whole row began to weep. Some audible, some not. None of us had any idea the reason the other was crying. It didn't matter. We were traveling through life together because we had prepared together. We were in an ancient ritual of enactment. We were in trance, and we could have gone back to Dogen's time or further—as far back as our own ancestors, as far back as the beginning of humanity.

Dokusan and Koan as Ritual

In shamanic journeying, the medicine person attends to the well-being of each individual in the ritual. They observe the participants so that the ritual meets the needs of the person in terms of transforming suffering into medicine. The shaman will offer various medicines or prescribe individual rituals within the larger ritual to enhance its effects. The shaman may direct the person to change which direction they are facing, to stand, to sit, to lie down. In essence, the individual is not left alone to create a false sense of ascension or awakening. It is an honor to work with the shaman in such a way.

In the view that Zen is shamanic and zazen is a shamanic experience, then the teacher is the leader of the ritual and the student is a ritual participant. Such a view changes the texture of the hierarchy within Zen from possibly oppressive to guiding and caring for those in the ritual or ceremony. Zen then looks less like training in the sense of making Zen students into teachers and more like a collaborative effort between leader and ritual participant, with the purpose of guiding the mind and body in a ritual of zazen through suffering into awakening.

Let's apply this view to the important practice of *dokusan* (also sometimes called sanzen or *daisan*), a smaller ritual within the group ritual of zazen. Dokusan is a face-to-face meeting with a guide, held in a private room. The intimate ritual of dokusan requires trust, integrity, and respect from both the ritual leader and the ritual participant. It functions through a holding and sharing face-to-face of zazen, the sacred medicine. Dokusan usually occurs during periods of zazen or at long sitting sessions. In this way, the guide and the person being guided connect under the influence of zazen. Under a state of mind brought by the ritual of zazen, the guiding teacher is able to see the practitioner's mind and help clear away obstructions to awakening.

A participant in the ritual of zazen doesn't simply walk up to the guiding teacher and ask for their time. A request must be made through an assistant, and the teacher then assesses whether or not the person is ready for the ritual of dokusan. Is the person ready to be guided into a deeper breath, or does the person need to remain in the ritual of zazen, accessing the stillness available? Or has the person requested an appointment outside of the realm of the ritual?

In contemporary times, the ritual aspect of dokusan can be misunderstood as stepping out of the ritual of zazen to have a conversation with the teacher. Even so, the effects of zazen may still be with the student in conversation. But without a sense of ritual, the conversation can dissolve into talk that intensifies suffering. Words exchanged in dokusan are meant to further the awakening stimulated with the strike of the match that lights the candles in the zendo. Conversation also is a different style of communication than the brief, sharp, intuitive exchange that is expected between guiding teacher and ritual participant under the influence of zazen.

At the time of dokusan, to maintain the ritual of zazen, the student sits waiting at the door. Sometimes a line of students sits in silence there. The guiding teacher rings the bell and the student responds with a bell, enters the room with the prescribed bows, and is seated. The sitting, ringing of the bell, and bowing are all rituals within the ritual of dokusan. As a guiding teacher myself, I discern and divine in witnessing the student do just those things. Before any words are exchanged, how the student has embodied the ritual of zazen is evident. Even the best of performers still cannot hide the truth, as their bodies reveal how the rituals are landing within. Ordained practitioners have more rituals of unfolding a bowing cloth, laying it down, bowing, and taking a seat, all while being observed. All these rituals represent opportunities to honor the Buddha through the teacher and prepare to receive the sacred teachings with respect.

I remember during my first years of Zen practice, while going through these steps, I would say to myself, "Wow, it takes a lot just to sit down." I thought this because I was trying to get to the teachers and did not yet know that the bowing and sitting down was the teaching. I did not yet understand that anything the guide said would be, at least in part, a response to my way of sitting and bowing. There were ritual actions, not merely the carrying out of instructions. It was shamanic in the sense that I was to remain in a state of consciousness in which I could barely speak. I remember many times just wanting to sit quietly in front of the teacher and simply exchange the eyes of zazen, witnessing the body of zazen through each other.

There is one teacher with whom I experienced this communion of zazen in dokusan. Upon being seated after bowing, we sat looking at each other for quite some time. Prior to that, I had been sitting in the zendo. When the teacher walked into the zendo, I asked myself, "Who is that?" I had been sitting with this teacher for two months by this time. That day, I didn't recognize him. He sat in the high dharma seat. He didn't speak a word for ten minutes. Then he bowed and left. Afterward, I was summoned to the abbot's cabin for dokusan. We sat looking eye-to-eye, absorbing the silence, experiencing the worldless guidance, and releasing nothing but tears from our human beingness. It was a trance state emerging from the nothingness and the non-doing of practice. I wasn't practicing. I wasn't a student, nor he a teacher. We were zazen. This experience marked for me again the shamanic nature of Zen. The experience was beyond Buddhism. The inquiry of life in that dokusan went thirty-thousand feet beneath the ground.

.   .   .

The ritual of dokusan can include the ritual of koan practice. Koan is an age-old encounter between a wisdom keeper and an aspirant seeking wisdom, when the mind and heart are to settle on a specific inquiry of life. A question is presented and a response is given, but more fundamentally, there are no answers to the riddles or stories presented by the guiding teacher. We are so used to answers that the koan practice stirs doubt for those who want to have all the answers. The questioning preserves the state of zazen and prevents idle conversation in dokusan. The guide shepherds the practitioner away from trying to create their own ascension or gate of realization and instead leaves the mind to squirm, stripped of intellect, allowing the expansion of zazen to take its course.

Although teachers across the various Zen schools have differing levels of interest in and experience with koans, intensive koan training is usually associated with Rinzai lineages. Like many Soto teachers, I have not been formally trained in koan practice, but I have been given the staff to lead others down the path and point to things along the way in the ritual of dokusan. Since dokusan, in my lineage, is a ritual reserved for and led by an abbot, abbess, or head teacher, others who hold one-on-one meetings use the term *practice discussion*. However, the ritual of dokusan is still the container for such discussions.

If you have not fully entered the path or committed to it, then there is no need for a guide. There is nothing for the guide to point to. At first, dokusan and koan rituals can seem off-putting, and there can be distrust in being led down a path that is unknown to you. A student at a Zen center once asked, "Why should I put my life in your hands?" I chuckled. I asked this person to not put his life in my hands. I asked him to simply walk alongside me, and we could talk a bit—but only if he felt a call to walk with me. I know underneath the concern was: how could he trust that I knew the way? There is no perfect direction in the walk of Zen. Everyone, the guide and the person being guided, will encounter the dips in the road—perhaps even falling off a cliff together. There is no one on the planet that completely knows what will be needed along the walk. Then, you may ask, how does one know to trust the guide? You must witness the guide walking others to and from. But most important is to have participated in the ritual of zazen so many times that you begin to recognize some of the road for yourself.

The impossible is possible. If we raise the ritual of zazen to its height, we can pierce the veil of this world. It is possible to see and hear things we have never imagined. We often speak of clarity, perhaps believing it has to do with whether or not we are confused about the things of the world. Clarity found in the ritual of zazen is the removal of obstructions from the spirit of body and mind. It is the removal of what might prevent you from seeing what's on the other side of the sky.

Chanting Spells

Chanting. No meaning. Just chanting. Listening to the bell. The wooden fish drum keeps time. No time. Sounds like water. Lost in the utterance with no meaning and no time. Only the vibration of voices from the chamber of our bones. Heart pounding its own rhythm. Not too fast, not too slow. Do not fall asleep. Someone is waiting. Someone you haven't met.

I experienced the oracle, the Black Angel Cards mentioned earlier in this text, that came into my life after intense chanting in the Nichiren tradition, as a "merging" with a dream. It included messages that existed before they came through me. Whether or not this experience was kensho, I had a glimpse of the source of things manifested in this world. Yet, I cannot explain this source. If I said the dream came from the ancestors, I don't know which particular ancestors. I know that the oracle came from deep concentration, which led to an experience not of my body nor mind. But even to say that feels like I know where the dream came from, and I do not. When I turned the oracle into a creation, a book of messages and a deck of cards with my artwork on them, I felt a sense of losing something unexplainable. That I had put a false ending to something larger than myself. However, the oracle born of chanting was also a beginning. It led to a divination process in which my seeing of life expanded my physical existence. I discovered that when we say we can be mirrors of each other, it is not that we see with the eye that we are one. Oneness, interrelationship, is an experience beyond our comprehension. Who and what is in the oneness? Who can say they know that which contains the whole universe?

Chanting is a powerful way to experience oneness. To merge our many voices as one sound is to join together in an intimate way as we do with our breath in sitting together. There is one mind, one heart. In his book *Zen Chants*, the Zen artist, translator, scholar, and teacher Kaz Tanahashi writes, "Zen chants are constant reminders that we practice together; we are one mind, one heart, one life. Even if we live or meditate alone, we are united with other awakened ones—not only with those in our immediate vicinity, but with all awakened beings from the past, present, and future, everywhere in the world."[1]

At dawn, the dark no longer able to hold back the light, the chanting begins. Few are excited. Some are barely awake, after having already sat several periods of zazen. Because we have walked from the zendo to the Buddha Hall, it may seem that we have left the ritual of zazen. But it remains in the approach to the chanting part of the ritual. Offerings are made, and we begin using our voices in a place where silence usually reigns. However, we will be using our voices in a different way. We will not be speaking our words. We will not be speaking of our suffering or joy. Mostly, we will utter sounds that are meant for the gods—sounds that can light up a dark cave if sung with our hearts. Sounds that will bring chills and tears.

To chant is to sing, and I have always been a singer. I sang in a gospel group called the Celestial Singers as a teenager. We were popular with our jazzy a capella style that would make the other teenagers swoon. In some places, our autographs were requested. We made an album of our songs and traveled by car to places to sing and share black poetry from the Harlem Renaissance. Although frightened to lead a song or sing alone at the time, I found the rising tide of the tones soothing when I heard my voice fuse with the others. One individual voice rising above another would have destroyed the relationship within the song. The singing was guaranteed to uplift everyone if we were of one mind and body.

When I entered the Nichiren tradition, I experienced the monotone Japanese-style of chanting as meditation through ancient sounds. I heard music. It was familiar to chant in the way that I had sung with all my body and mind. To access the energy of the body through the voice was to move suffering into wellness. Eventually, I also led the drum and songs in Lakota Sundance ceremonies, where again, the gathering of my energy through my body brought healing.

Music from the church and music heard in the black community have their roots in Africa, where music and chants were and are used to heal entire communities. In African ceremony, the singing and drumming create the atmosphere needed to move a prayer into being. In early times, when outsiders came and observed the abundance of dancing and singing in African cultures, it was reduced to the view, "Africans like to sing and dance." There was no understanding that the music was a conduit in the ritual of prayer—that the people were in ceremony.

In Zen, we sometimes misunderstand the chanting as something other than part of the ritual of zazen. It becomes another thing to do. With that frame of mind, the chanting, unfelt, becomes shallow. The monotone in Zen chanting can be mistaken as not needing to bring energy to each syllable, each sound. Many are reluctant to chant, as it has been rendered meaningless to them. Perhaps they find comfort in just sitting without any rituals. If so, it might be wise to assess whether Soto Zen, with its chanting, bowing, and making offerings, is for you.

There have been many efforts to assist in embracing Zen chants such as scoring the chants to music or changing them. The temple founded by the late Zen master, Jiyu Kennett, for instance, adapted the chants into a style of Gregorian chanting. Rev. Kanho Yakushiji, a monk at Ikkyu-ji in Kyoto, Japan, who is also a musician, has adapted chants to music using string instruments, electric drums, choruses, and more. His videos can be found on YouTube. He said he worried whether or not his elders would approve, but they did.

According to Stephen P. Slottow, the author of *The Americanization of Zen Chanting*, "The North American acculturation of Zen Buddhism has been characterized by two opposing tendencies: a conservative desire to keep practices 'pure' and unadulterated (in some cases, an idealized and simplified projection of 'pure') versus the urge to 'Americanize,' that is, to individualize and innovate to fit changing contemporary North American contexts and musical norms." He also notes, and I paraphrase, that Zen Buddhism has influenced jazz musicians such as Keith Jarrett, Western composers such as John Cage, shakuhachi [flute] music, new age, and "mood" music, where it is used as a slightly faded exotic synonym for "relaxation."[2] If it is calming music, folks in the general population call this "Zen" because, as Slottow infers, much of the music in the realm of calm has been influenced by Zen Buddhism. But Zen chants have a deeper purpose than calming one's nerves.

Often the inward gaze in sitting meditation, such as zazen, can surface pain and suffering. There is help. Even while we are sitting still in meditation, there is a constant rhythm in our bodies that can be accessed to assist in navigating the emerging waves of suffering. The heart is beating, the blood is flowing. Cells are rejuvenating themselves. In this sense, there is movement in the stillness of sitting just as there is stillness in the movement of chanting.

As Zen is an embodied experience, chanting interacts with the movement of the body. Chanting is a chance to turn outward while remaining in zazen. It gathers the energy needed to continue the inward illumination. Tanahashi writes, "Chanting together in full voice, with everyone's mind and heart pointed outward, is a dynamic, energizing activity that encourages us in our commitment and dedication to practice." I add, it helps to sustain and be present in the rituals and ceremonies. Tanahashi goes on to say, "The recited texts can also be repeated in stillness and silence [in our heart and mind], reminding us of our understanding, vow, and commitment. Thus, Zen chants shape our meditation, consciousness, and life activities."[3]

Accessing the one body and one mind, as is possible in Zen chanting, I am certain comes from much earlier—

from the beginning of humanity, when the first sound was uttered. For example, Hinduism used these ancient sounds to create mantras and sounds that help connect to the universe, which we are. The most popular is the mantra OM or AUM, which is said to be the basic sound of the universe. Chanting OM is to connect to ourselves, through body and mind, as nature. OM is chanted in many secular spiritual circles and in many religious traditions, including in some Buddhist traditions. The OM mantra appears as part of a few Zen chants, but it is not usually chanted alone. However, the profound and nourishing effect of chanting OM is recognized in Zen as well.

In Zen chanting, the *kokyo*, a person who leads the chants, calls out the name of the chant. Others in the *doanryo* ring the large *keisu* temple bell and play the *mokugyo*, a large fish-shaped drum. Then everyone's voice joins in unison with the tone set by the kokyo. It reminds me of when, in African, Native American, and Islamic traditions, the call is sung out before everyone joins in the song of prayer. I consider the kokyo's announcement in Zen chanting as a call to our spirits to awaken and to listen. The call from the kokyo must be resonant, with deep breaths in and out, so it is simultaneously felt in the body of the kokyo and the assembly. Far from this kind of cultivated, adept breathing, most of us today do not even have a baseline of healthy breathing. The popular book *Breath: The New Science of a Lost Art*, by James Nestor, basically says we don't know how to breathe. We have ignored the purpose of the nose and have become mouth breathers, which has caused all kinds of health problems. Those who call us out to awaken must themselves be able to breathe. I want to share an ancient

Chinese stone inscription (from the Zhou dynasty, circa 500 BCE) included at the front of Nestor's book:

> In transporting the breath, the inhalation must be full. When it is full, it has big capacity. When it has big capacity, it can be extended. When it is extended, it can penetrate downward. When it penetrates downward, it will become calmly settled. When it is calmly settled, it will be strong and firm. When it is strong and firm, it will germinate. When it germinates, it will grow. When it grows, it will retreat upward. When it retreats upward, it will reach the top of the head. The secret power of Providence moves above. The secret power of the Earth moves below.
>
> He who follows this will live. He who acts against this will die.[4]

The breath from the soft area of the belly, from the *hara* as we say in Zen, brings forth life energy—the qi or chi, as described in qigong, or prana as described in yoga traditions. Hara is the Japanese word for "lower abdomen," and we are taught to breathe from the hara in zazen. Placing attention here also helps us to take in the chant and feel the power of it as our own. Breathing into the soft belly helps call in resonant vibration, healing deep in the gut. The deep awareness that builds there can focus and strengthen life force.

It is as important to prepare our bodies for chanting as much as many of us do for sitting. If the body is ready, the chants can work at a far deeper level than merely saying each word correctly. Chanting, singing, or hearing music, when infused with the medicine of spirit and nature, increases life force.

Zen has specific chants to encourage compassion, awakening, loving-kindness, wisdom beyond wisdom (which is insight), and boundlessness. In these states, the experience of oneness while chanting can be carried throughout your life. Tanahashi writes, "When we experience a sense of oneness with other individuals near and far, as well as with other living and nonliving beings, we are drawn toward selfless and compassionate states of mind."[5] It is an example of continuous practice.

An important chant that occurs every day in some Zen centers, during ordinations, and at full moon (Fusatsu) ceremonies is the chant for atonement (or repentance). To atone is to acknowledge any places we have broken our connection to each other and to the earth. Atonement is not about feeling guilty but about caring and valuing life. In his book *Returning to Silence*, Dainin Katagiri Roshi says that repentance in Buddhism means perfect openness of heart. He writes, "If we open ourselves completely . . . we are ready to listen to the voiceless voice of the universe." He explains, "The ritual of repentance is not to ask forgiveness from someone for what one has done."[6] With atonement, we open our hearts, which enables the ceremonies and rituals to take place with full attention and presence. It clears the field for the intended illumination. The traditional Zen atonement chant is said three times:

> All my ancient twisted karma
> from beginningless, greed, hate, and delusion
> born of body, speech, and mind—
> I now fully avow.

This ancient Chinese verse, which is from the Flower Splendor Sutra, emphasizes actions from the beginningless. Even though it says "my" twisted karma, when we chant for atonement, we are going beyond our individual lives. We atone for our ancestors and for all human beings who have ever lived. This ceremony of clearing, especially when done on the full moon, is to ask for a chance to begin again. It is to ask for an understanding that, as human beings, the effects of our actions are not always in the realm of wellness. If we maintain beginner's mind, we do not have to begin again. We are always in atonement with all our actions.

Are we praying when we chant? Is there divinity? I say yes, but not in the sense of praying to one God, Creator, Great Spirit, Father, or Mother, or to many gods. We are not praying to Shakyamuni Buddha, who was not a deity or god but a man who walked the earth in flesh and bones. The prayer is in the sound made to the universe. It is innate in the states of consciousness being espoused and the awakening being called forth by each chant. It is not a request for things made from our own minds, which have limited capacity to call in all that we need for wellness. Like our minds calling on particular things for our lives rather than chanting *into* an enlightened consciousness. Zen chants translated to English may have the problem of something of the ancient being lost in translation. There have been great efforts to revise English translations of Zen chants to capture the original intent of the Japanese and Sino-Japanese language, yet it is difficult to do so while retaining accessibility. For this reason, and for the sake of gathering the shamanic bones of Zen, I put my attention on the untranslatable *dharanis* or "chanting spells" as I like to call them.

Zen Spells or Dharanis

Much like the African and Native drumming I have done over the years, dharanis range in tone and rhythm. These chants are mystical in nature. They may have the same effect as a mantra, but they are not one phrase or word. They are verses taken from longer sacred texts, and the dharanis have a more specific purpose than chants intended to stimulate a certain state of consciousness. A dharani is an incantation that can serve as a talisman of protection. Dharanis, by the force and rhythm of their sounds, are meant to move mountains.

If the idea of chanting spells in Buddhism sounds wrong to you, that is likely because, until recently, modern scholars have neglected the scale and importance of such spells in Buddhist history. In *Buddhist Magic*, Sam van Schaik tries to redress this situation by providing information on dharanis:

> Spells are found, or at least mentioned in passing, in many Mahayana sutras. In this context, they are often called dharanis. One of the best-known examples is the dharani chapter of the *Lotus Sutra*. . . . It follows a format that had already been established by the spell literature of mainstream Buddhism, in which the Buddha teaches a spell, or calls on one of his followers to teach it and then enumerates its benefits. . . .
> Alongside the famous sutras of Mahayana Buddhism such as the *Perfection of Wisdom* and the *Lotus Sutra*, a vast literature developed around dharanis. Though they are rarely considered equally important, they were probably the most copied, recited, and well circulated Buddhist texts.[7]

Zen dharanis, which often have roots in Vajrayana Buddhism and before that Vedic mantras, originated as magical spells against spirits and demons. As Buddhist scholar and author Richard D. McBride writes, "Numerous gods, beings, spirits, and creatures that populated the Hindu and Buddhist pantheons and pan-Indian cosmology were introduced in various stages into China first and then into Korea and Japan, where they merged with the animistic beliefs of local peoples and eventually came to dominate East Asian demonology."[8]

These events in the history of Buddhism remind me of how when enslaved Africans were introduced to the Christian tradition, they merged the rituals and songs of Christianity with ancient African spirituality. One of these rituals was baptism, which resonated with ancient African beliefs about the use of water for purification from misconceptions and in unification with God or nature through water burials. Although they were forced by slave merchants and owners to go against their so-called "heathen ways" and bow down to this new god, the merging of animistic beliefs of Africa into this enforced religion changed how the enslaved prayed and survived. I imagine the dharani, similar to baptism in Christianity, helped those who practiced chanting spells for various reasons in indigenous traditions to embrace Buddhism.

It is said that the dharani is a Buddhist response to Vedic and Hindu mantras. With Buddhism's transmission to China, notes McBride, "Chinese practitioners embraced these efficacious incantations and seamlessly amalgamated them with traditional Chinese spell procedures," using terms such as "spells," "spirit spells," and "spell techniques or spell-craft."[9] Through the wish-fulfilling spells or by carrying the spell on their person as a talisman, protection could be achieved from ghosts and demons. When, several centuries later, esoteric or tantric (Vajrayana) Buddhism entered China, ritualists began also to use the word *mantra* to refer to these spells. In the end, the dharanis became the chants to protect folks from harm of all kinds. As noted in the "Dharani Sutras" entry in *Brill's Encyclopedia of Buddhism*, "Protection is promised from all sorts of conceivable threats: humans, nonhumans, . . . sorcery, demons, poison, weapons, sickness, fever, possession, epidemics, weakness, snakebite, spells, magical bonds, wizardry, fire, water, obstacles, great dangers, calamities, drought, floods, thunderbolts, dispute, bad dreams, bad rebirth, bad omens, bad constellations, physical defects, sorrow, the evil eye, royal power and punishment, thieves, robbers, armies, war, famine, earthquake, meteors, untimely death, insects, worms, wild animals, the loss of vital fluid, and so forth."[10]

It was thought that, if one chants a dharani, the body becomes firm as a *vajra*, which is a Tibetan Buddhist ritual weapon symbolizing the properties of a diamond and a thunderbolt. Ensuring the power of the dharani, an altar must be erected with objects and deities that invoke what is being called forth in the dharani.

An altar is always at the center of any shamanic practice. Therefore, altars throughout the temple are always ready to invoke each chant, whether it is a dharani or not. In Zen as practiced by ancient Chinese and Japanese monastics, each verse of a dharani was considered mystic. Tanahashi writes, "Sometimes teachers of Esoteric Buddhism assert that chanting dhāranīs, which are beyond intellectual understanding, is an essential way to experience the indescribable heart of the Buddha."[11] Some mantras or dharanis were originally composed of "nonsense" syllables, intended for the efficacy of their sounds rather than meaning. Even for those that can be translated, however, it is worth considering whether that is always a good idea. To not translate these verses is to maintain the esoteric and shamanic nature of the chants and to sustain the secret medicine within them.

On the other hand, translating the dharanis allows access to their verbal meaning. *The Great Compassionate Heart Dharani*, for instance, has been translated by Tanahashi and Roshi Joan Halifax. In the dharani *The Mystical Blue-Necked One*, Avalokiteshvara (a version of Guan Yin) is invoked and grants all wishes, overcomes obstacles, and purifies delusion. Even the ancient mantra Oм appears in the dharani. Here is Tanahashi and Roshi Halifax's translation of the *The Mystical Blue-Necked One Avalokiteshvara or the Great Compassionate Heart Dharani*:

Homage to the Three Treasures.
Homage to noble Avalokiteshvara,
noble Bodhisattva Mahasattva,
who embodies great compassion.
Oм. Homage to you
who protect all those who are fearful.
Being one with you,
the Blue-necked noble Avalokiteshvara,
I bring forth your radiant heart that grants all wishes,
    overcomes obstacles, and purifies delusion.

Here is the mantra:

Om. You are luminous with shining wisdom.
You transcend the world.
O, Lion King, great bodhisattva.
Remember, remember, this heart.
Act, act. Realize, realize. Continue, continue.
Victor, great victor. Maintain, maintain.
Embodiment of freedom.
Arise, arise, the immaculate one, the undefiled
    being.
Advance, advance. You are supreme on this earth.
You remove the harm of greed.
You remove the harm of hatred.
You remove the harm of delusion.
Lion King, remove, remove all defilements.
The universal lotus grows from your navel.
Act, act. Cease, cease. Flow, flow. Awake, awake.
Compassionate one, enlighten, enlighten.
Blue-necked one,
You bring joy to those who wish to see clearly.
    Svaha.
You succeed. Svaha. You greatly succeed. Svaha.
You have mastered the practice. Svaha.
Blue-necked one. Svaha.
Boar-faced one, lion-faced one. Svaha.
You hold the lotus. Svaha.
You hold the blade wheel. Svaha.
You liberate through the sound of the conch.
    Svaha.
You hold a great staff. Svaha.

You are the dark conqueror
abiding near the left shoulder. Svaha.
You wear a tiger skin. Svaha.
Homage to the Three Treasures.
Homage to noble Avalokiteshvara. Svaha.
Realize all phrases of this mantra. Svaha.[12]

It was discovered later by Tanahashi. (The dharani of *The Mystical Blue-Necked One Avalokiteshvara* was originally translated into English by renowned Zen teacher, D. T. Suzuki in 1950.) Avalokiteshvara is recognized as having taken the form of the Hindu god Shiva, which makes clear the intersection of Zen chanting with the ancient chanting of Hinduism. In China, it was written that not only did Avalokiteshvara appear as Shiva, he also took on the ash-painted and matted hair appearance of a Naga sadhu or sannyasi of India, ascetics who worship Shiva. Naga Sannyasis, with their huge and long Rudraksha malas, are similar to the hermit monks of ancient Chinese Buddhism and were, along with the ancient diviners/seers of Africa, among the first monks in the world. Since there are Naga sadhus who are female—perhaps the first Indian nuns before Buddhism—I would add that Avalokiteshvara might appear as female and take the form of the goddess Shakti instead of the male Shiva.

. :.

Has the medicine been lost in the translation of some of the dharanis? The way the medicine might have entered the body has certainly changed. Yet I believe the secret remains in the original sound of the voice—not the words—of the monk who chants from the mind of kensho. The medicine remains in the chanting of the shaman, of the radiant one(s) who created the dharani, the spell, or the talisman.

The most chanted dharani in contemporary Western Zen centers may be the *Dai Hi Shin Dharani*. It is meant to attend to the heart—not only a personal heart but also the great heart of all humanity. It is especially good for times when we collectively suffer from illness, unsurmountable death, corruption, extensive killing in hate crimes, war, and other catastrophes. The *Shosaimiyo Kichijo Dharani* is another popular dharani chanted in Zen centers that is considered a spell for averting calamities.

When I first saw the *Dai Hi Shin Dharani*, I felt that I would never be able to memorize all the words. They were so strange. But I had learned the words to Lakota songs, so I tried. I would take the chant to my room and try to repeat and keep the words in my mind. By the time I returned to chant it with the sangha, my mind would fail me. Finally, I put the chant book down and began listening. Eventually, I could say a few lines. Then out of the blue, I noticed a rhythm. It was like listening to a drum rhythm bringing energy. I caught the rhythm in my body and the words flowed.

Once, there was a pregnant woman attending a practice period. She gave birth in a hospital and brought the baby back to the monastery for the rest of the practice period. The baby was crying and annoyed one day. I knew the *Dai Hi Shin Dharani* had been repeatedly chanted during the pregnancy. So, I thought to try an experiment. I got close to the baby and chanted. The baby suddenly stopped crying. It had heard those sacred sounds before and was immediately calm and focused by the chanting.

I offer, here, the *Chant of Great Compassionate Mind,* the *Dai Hi Shin Dharani,* as chanted at the San Francisco Zen Center. Our lives are so uncertain and often troubled. I thought this gift may bring calm to you, as it did the baby. If it calms you, it at once brings calm to the hearts of all humanity. There are many recordings online of this dharani. The vowels are the same as that of the Spanish language. Write it down or use a small calligraphy brush to copy it, and keep it close to your person. May it bring peace to you and others:

NAMU KARA TAN NO TORA YA YA NAMU ORI YA BORYO KI CHI SHIFU RA YA FUJI SATO BO YA MOKO SATO BO YA MO KO KYA RUNI KYA YA EN SA HARA HA EI SHU TAN NO TON SHA NAMU SHIKI RI TOI MO ORI YA BORYO KI CHI SHIFU RA RIN TO BO NA MU NO RA KIN JI KI RI MO KO HO DO SHA MI SA BO O TO JO SHU BEN O SHU IN SA BO SA TO NO MO BO GYA MO HA TE CHO TO JI TO EN O BO RYO KI RU GYA CHI KYA RYA CHI I KIRI MO KO FUJI SA TO SA BO SA BO MO RA MO RA MO KI MO KI RI TO IN KU RYO KU RYO KE MO TO RYO TO RYO HO JA YA CHI MO KO HO JA YA CHI TO RA TO RA CHIRI NI SHIFU RA YA SHA RO SHA RO MO MO HA MO RA HO CHI RI YUKI YUKI SHI NO SHI NO ORA SAN FURA SHA RI HA ZA HA ZA FURA SHA YA KU RYO KU RYO MO RA KU RYO KU RYO KI RI SHA RO SHA RO SHI RI SHI RI SU RYO SU RYO FUJI YA FUJI YA FUDO YA FUDO YA MI CHIRI YA NORA KIN JI CHIRI SHUNI NO HOYA MONO SOMO KO SHIDO YA SOMO KO MOKO SHIDO YA SOMO KO SHIDO YU KI SHIFU RA YA SOMO KO NORA KIN JI SOMO KO MO RA NO RA SOMO KO SHIRA SU

OMO GYA YA SOMO KO SOBO MOKO SHIDO YA SOMO KO SHAKI
RA OSHI DO YA SOMO KO HODO MOGYA SHIDO YA SOMO KO
NORA KIN JI HA GYARA YA SOMO KO MO HORI SHIN GYARA
YA SOMO KO NAMU KARA TAN NO TORA YA YA NAMU ORI
YA BORYO KI CHI SHIFU RA YA SOMO KO SHITE DO MODO
RA HODO YA SO MO KO

Rituals of
Celebration
and Initiation

I bow as my dharma sister slowly shaves my head, alongside two other novitiates. One patch at a time. The cool air whips against the baldness, except for a tiny, tight, nearly invisible curl at the top. Together, we chant for bodhisattvas and mahasattvas to concentrate their hearts on us. We leave to bathe. We return and enter the zendo together in new ceremonial clothes to accept the robe of liberation. It's cold sitting with only a juban, kimono, two layers from our new underwear. We are babies about to be born.

During my first role as co-teacher at a Zen center, I was invited to lead the Parinirvana ceremony, a short, sweet, ritual-filled honoring of the teachings Buddha gave toward the end of his life. Before the ritual, I was thinking about what it meant to be a Zen teacher. I was feeling proud and unsure. By the time the procession of teachers and others lined up behind me, my mind stopped and something else took over—something hard to articulate, something that would be missed if I had not accepted the offer to lead.

There was a long procession into the zendo. I was seated in a high, antique Chinese chair. I wore ceremonial white slippers on my feet and a white robe beneath my black one. I laid out my bowing cloth to protect the robe of liberation from the dirt on the floor. I carried the traditional fly whisk (*hossu*), a wand-like stick with animal hair. I waved the whisk. In waving the whisk, I knew in my bones that

I was performing an ancient and shamanic act of clearing the space for the ceremony and for possible awakening. In ancient times, the hair on the whisk was a deer tail or, in Tibet, hair from the tail of an ox. Today, the whisk is made of horsehair. A practical use of the whisk is to send away small flying insects so that they will not be harmed in the ritual. Therefore, the waving of the wand is also to protect life. In some traditions, there is the *shubi*, which is a whisk with the hair of a stag. Like the hossu, it is used for those who lead disciples, as a stag is the leader of deer. In many African traditions, the priests carry horsehair whisks, much like the one I was carrying in the Parinirvana ceremony. The use of horsehair has symbolic and spiritual meanings in many ancient shamanic cultures. I feel the varied hairs of different animals, especially the horse, have more meaning in Zen than what has been transmitted. My guess is these animals—the deer, ox, and horse—were prominent in the survival and protection of the people. Perhaps, in some instances, they were integral to their mythology and spiritual beliefs.

It is my view that the horsehair is integral to the ceremony I was leading. In the *Shobogenzo* (*Treasury of the True Dharma Eye*), Dogen Zenji teaches about the Parinirvana Sutra, the sutra that is the basis of the Parinirvana ceremony. He highlights the whip as a symbol of death in a story about four horses that appears in the sutra. The four horses are used as metaphors to represent different responses to our lives. The first horse is very intelligent, but when it sees the whip coming, it is startled. The second horse is disturbed when the whip lightly grazes its mane. The third horse is shocked when the whip hits its flesh. The fourth horse is awakened when the whip cuts through to the bone. The core of these teachings is the exhortation to awaken before the "whip" of death or impermanence penetrates to the bone. When teachers lead the Parinirvana ceremony, they are enacting an awakening to the reality that there is a shadow of death in our lives. To ignore it—going about our daily lives being intelligent but not wise—is to live with blinders on. This understanding keeps the leading of such a ceremony out of the realm of ego and places it in the unseen and vast experience of awakening.

In the ceremony of awakening to death, I also carried a *kotsu* (also known as *nyo-i*), a short (eleven to twelve inches) staff or scepter, sometimes symbolized as a bone relic or the spine of a human being. When a person is bowing, the staff is held horizontal over the earth. Some ceremony leaders place the staff in a vertical position and tap the earth. The staff's use as a ceremonial tool can be found in almost every ancient culture. It is often used by those with authority; in the Zen tradition, it is carried by those who have been given transmission to teach and lead a sangha. In this way, Zen follows the traditions of indigenous cultures. Staffs are carried by chiefs in many indigenous traditions, including African and Native American. Their staffs are usually more embellished than the Zen kotsu and are also often much longer, at least five to six feet, exuding great authority with their feathers, trinkets, and medicine. The longer length of such staffs also allows them to touch the earth. This warns small animals away to protect them from harm—the protective aspect of the ceremonial tool, as with the Zen whisk. Also, like in Zen, the staff is used to send ceremonial prayers into the earth. This is how I experience holding my kotsu.

The one carrying the hossu (whisk) and the kotsu (staff) might be mistaken as a high, holy, superior figure. I see the one carrying these ritual tools as the one who goes first and uses the tools on behalf of the assembled to set the tone of the ritual, make the offerings, and see that all is well before the ceremony begins.

As I stood before the altar in leading the Parinirvana ceremony, with attendants and teachers supporting, the silence took over. Evening had descended, and there was a profound sense of death penetrating my bones. I bowed deeply to the teaching coming through without a word uttered.

· ·

Zen rituals and ceremonies can appear odd, fussy, busy, and unnecessary, if not ridiculous to some. As the result of the shamanic aspect of Zen going unrecognized in contemporary times, it is difficult to understand what is going on. Think back to any ceremony or ritual in your life, strip it of its roots, and what you see are folks doing strange things, singing strange songs, and appearing under the influence of a script or something external to them. This distorted view can arise because Zen rituals and ceremonies aren't meant to be *observed* but to be *engaged*. They are meant to engage one's whole body and mind as expressions of zazen. In essence, you cannot "feel the spirit" unless you have given yourself over to the expansiveness being created. If not, then the rituals and ceremonies are far too abstract. If the rituals and ceremonies are done without soul and spirit, or just wholehearted presence, they become another routine, one more thing to do in the way of the world. If you are not available for what may come through engaging the mind and body, then the time spent is merely time spent.

In engaging Zen ritual and ceremony, you must enter the door. Only in this way can it be revealed that there is no door and there is not even a way. It took time for me to go from witnessing strange activities in Zen, to stumbling through the rituals and ceremonies, to finally engaging in them in my own way, in what I experienced as "working the medicine." The engagement came alive for me in discovering its shamanistic elements. Given there is little spoken about these elements, I was surprised to find so many documents, books, scholars, and Zen teachers supporting that there is a foundation for engaging the unseen and mystical within Zen.

In a divine Zen, I can engage Zen in every moment. Not the external Zen of people, places, and ideas about being Buddhist. Not absoluteness or relativism. Something much broader and more profound than the idea of Zen, ritual, ceremony, or even shamanism. The rituals and ceremonies are avenues not only to breathing as a mundane act but also to the physicality of life.

It is important to speak of the effects of the rituals and ceremonies but with the understanding that experiences are different across culture, ethnicity, gender, class, physical ability, depth of ceremonial experience, and so forth. The complexities and multidimensional aspects of every human being influence the outcome of ritual and ceremony. There is something internal to the experience of the rituals. "Zen ritual can give rise to Zen mind," writes the scholar Dale S. Wright. "In the act of participation, we sense and understand something that we will otherwise miss altogether. In order to appreciate the ritual dimension of Zen practice, therefore, we must move beyond describing these ceremonies in order to consider what they are and why Zen Buddhists might engage in them."[1]

Beginner's mind is central to every ritual and ceremony. It is not the mind of starting something, although one's first experience at anything is a touchtone for accessing beginner's mind. It is not beginning again. Beginner's mind is not knowing. Not knowing never ends. To constantly be in the not knowing is to discover life over and over. Zen rituals and ceremonies sustain the unknown. Even if you discover something, it is quickly replaced with uncertainty.

THE CEREMONY OF SESSHIN

The deepest time of diving into the unknown is during sesshins—five to nine days of sitting six to eight hours a day. Most newcomers are frightened away by sitting still quietly for such long hours. Many see the sesshin as something to endure as opposed to a chance to enter a ceremony of experiencing life from the body and the breath, despite the busy mind. I often suggest allowing the schedule to hold you rather than you hold the schedule. You can't hold the whole sesshin in your small mind because it is much bigger than you. You can't hold a ceremony alone that is meant for a collective body. Instead, if you experience each moment, each breath, each feeling or emotion in the silence, in the bowing, and in the chanting, you come to see that it is not about you or the worldly skills you use to manage your life. It's much larger.

The most popular sesshin is Rohatsu. Rohatsu sesshin marks the annual celebration of Buddha's enlightenment, which in the Zen tradition is thought to be on the eighth day of the twelfth lunar month. It is one of the largest worldwide Zen ceremonies, and practitioners fully engage the ritual of zazen for eight days. The schedule includes hours of sitting meditation and ceremonies, including the daily ritual of *oryoki*, a ritual of eating that maintains the silence and stillness of the sesshin.

The first time I encountered this sesshin, I noticed a sudden hush in the center for at least the week before. Inner preparation went on within all who would attend. Those new to Rohatsu, like myself, were silenced by fear of the unknown. Those not so new were anchoring themselves, without effort, in the silence they had honed over the years. We were headed for a deep dive that everyone, whether new or old to the ceremony, had the chance to surrender to—and had no idea of what would become of them if they did. Some Zen center residents have learned to wade on the surface of the ritual, taking a vacation from the hard work found in Zen practice. Some drop in thinking they know what will happen. Others have no idea of what they have said yes to. The latter group enters the ceremony with beginner's mind, which can lead to being surprised by the wisdom hidden within.

The hidden jewels of life can be found in the smell, sound, touch, and tastes of oryoki—a ritual of eating. In this ritual, the roles of being a giver, receiver, and gift (the food) are enacted between servers and those being served. Oryoki is zazen in motion. It teaches participants how to use silence and the breath to see one's life while performing prescribed activities. First, three tiny bowls are filled with a morsel of food to be offered to the ancestor, Buddha. The head of the kitchen leads a chant in blessing the food and all those who helped, but mostly to offer gratitude. The three tiny bowls on a tray are carried to where the meal is to take place, where the assembly bows with the head of the kitchen and witnesses the offering to Buddha at the altar.

To maintain the silence of the ritual, servers and receivers use hand gestures during the meal. Learning the gestures is a first step but using deep intuition honed in zazen is the foundation by which the giving and receiving are ceremonially done without speaking a word. Oryoki feels like an hour-long silent dance between participant and server. If the server can sense the needs of the participants and the participants are aware of what is needed to nourish the body *in the moment the server arrives*, the ritual of oryoki can be of benefit to the ceremony of the sesshin and to dealing with real-life challenges, individually and collectively. During my first oryoki ritual, I sobbed like a baby when the teachers came by and served the students. I had never been served in such a way. Their dance was much lighter than the students, and their intuition was deeper in knowing exactly how much to place in the bowls without a word uttered.

There are as many challenges in the ritual of oryoki as there are rituals within the ritual—the folding and unfolding of a variety of cloths, the order and placement of bowls and eating utensils, bowing, chanting, the washing of bowls while seated, and more. One can go into mental paralysis, lose one's appetite, or sob. For me, the teachings came through in the sweet sobbing and the challenges. The ritual revealed what wasn't shown in sitting still without oryoki. There was a chance to discover how we suffer and how we express such suffering. One can realize the emotions and feelings arising in the sesshin are in response to past life experiences even though they are being stimulated by the ritual. Discovering how grief, rage, or loneliness may take your breath away in the middle of eating soup can lead to amazing insight about these emotions in your daily life. In essence, the mirror of oryoki can be transformative.

Toward the end of the oryoki ritual, we set aside tiny grains of rice for the hungry spirits. We wash our bowls, and some of the water is saved to be offered as ambrosia water to the ancestors. We wrap our sacred bowls in the reverse order from when we unwrapped them to eat. Wooden clackers struck by the kokyo (chant leader) signal different chants and phases of the meal, and the chanting brings the ritual into the heart.

After day three or four of any sesshin, most participants will have lost track of themselves, of time and space. Such an experience has occurred for many in shamanic journeys. The expansion that occurs in Zen ritual and ceremony is undeniably not of this world, even though we are physically still in the world. The opening to the vastness of life continues day by day throughout the sesshin, unless fear, exhaustion from not preparing, or boredom takes over. Coffee or tea may keep your body going, but are you present? Do the stimulating beverages keep you tense, unable to release? Have you eaten too much for a time in which you are mostly sitting and need little food? These are the practical questions to ask when surviving ceremony.

Often there are ceremonies within the ceremony of sesshin. During Rohatsu at the San Francisco Zen Center, there are two Shunryu Suzuki Roshi memorials honoring the founder's life and teachings. Early in the morning on those days, there is making offerings, chanting, and bowing at the altar in his honor. Also, on one of the memorial days, priests talk to Suzuki Roshi's spirit, telling him of their love and how things are going. Speaking to the ancestors in such a way is part of many earth-based practices, in which I include Zen and other Buddhist traditions.

On the eighth day, there is a ceremonial celebration of Buddha's enlightenment to culminate Rohatsu. Chanting practitioners circumambulate the Buddha Hall amid the intense energy of taiko drums. Once while drumming on the taiko drums during the celebration, along with a fellow drum medicine woman, I felt as though I was flying. My hands were leading the rhythm as if I had played it for a million years. The smell of incense filled the hall and flowers were tossed in the air. This celebration is an extension of the ritual of sesshin and it is a celebration of zazen as well. In essence, it is the day when we celebrate a practice that has helped us so much in seeing our lives. That said, I notice many find it hard to play and laugh during this time, after eight days of sitting. Some have done the celebration of Buddha's enlightenment so many times, it has lost its meaning and they are merely doing what is expected of them. If one's heart is not engaged in the ritual or ceremony, then attending may only cause suffering. No one should feel forced into ceremony but rather called to it.

After the eight days of my first Rohatsu sesshin, I noticed that my body was relaxed where there is usually muscle tension. I was calm, yes, but there was more to it than that—I felt myself to be more than the body I inhabited, and I could see that those around me were not who they were before we started. I had gone through some of the pain and suffering I carried, walked through the waves with the breath during sitting meditation. The unknown had not gobbled me up. Instead, it landed me on the shore across from where I had been living in pain. When I walked out the door into the busy streets, it was clear that, though I was on the same planet where I had suffered, I had found a new place inside me to live.

With every sesshin, from that time forward, I would continuously land in places within me I never knew existed. I experienced this as shamanic transformation and imagined others were going through it as well. Most rituals and ceremonies in the world have guidelines or protocols to ensure a safe journey. You may feel as though there is nothing to rely upon once you have been shifted from one place to another through ceremony. For that reason, I created and eventually shared with others a protocol for before, during, and after an extended Buddhist retreat or sesshin. Those guidelines are at the back of this book.

The Ritual of Sewing and the Ceremony of Taking Vows

After practicing for years, including many journeys in Rohatsu, I was invited to enter lay initiation by taking vows as a lay practitioner. For me, this would involve a nine-month process with my teacher, which included studying texts as well as sewing what is called a *rakusu*—a five-panel short robe worn around the neck, looking like a well-tailored bib. Not everyone goes through a nine-month process, and some may not sew their own rakusu for various reasons. But I'm glad I did, as it was through the ritual of sewing that I understood the precepts of being aware of killing, stealing, lying, intoxication, sexual harm, and other ways we do not honor our lives and the lives of others. I accepted the invitation as a path of forgiveness.

My teacher was considered the master Zen sewing teacher in the country, and she trained many others to teach the ritual of sewing. The rakusu comes in many pieces of cloth that need to be stitched together in a precise pattern. With each of the hundreds of stitches, a verse is chanted to maintain a mind-heart of zazen. NAMU KIE BUTSU, NAMU KIE HO, NAMU KIE SO. Pause. Then again, NAMU KIE BUTSU, NAMU KIE HO, NAMU KIE SO. Pause. Like many initiatory rituals in shamanic or indigenous traditions, sewing can be a way to become aware of mind consciousness. We can observe the mind going between expansion and restriction with each stitch of Buddha's robe of liberation. It is a practice to return us home, to the place we belong, which is our original nature of awareness and awakening. As the stitches are interrelated to form a rakusu, we are interrelated, forming a world. There is no way of separating the interrelationship without destroying the fabric of life. In this sense, the ritual of sewing, like all rituals and ceremonies of Zen, mimics life. Through silent engagement with needle, thread, cloth, breath, and body, we can understand the most profound teachings.

A stunning aspect of this sewing is that, once done, the majority of practitioners have no idea how to sew a rakusu. It isn't that they failed at learning; they were absorbed in a process beyond the mere act of sewing—but this is not known until after the sewing is done. Sewing is a walk with habitual worry, frustration, anger, desire to give up, efforts to be perfect, competition, and the surfacing of old trauma within the body. But mostly the frustration of not knowing can wreak havoc on one's nerves. The ritual of sewing turns out not to be a course of learning how to sew a rakusu or Buddha's robe per se. It is a ritual of transformation and liberation, from pieces to the whole, from relative angst to absolute peace with whatever the outcome. At the same time, it is a ritual of no outcome.

In most cases, friends and community are invited to put in a few stitches, as a reminder that you are not practicing for yourself. Once the rakusu is complete, it is given back to the sewing teacher and then to your particular teacher, who will conduct a small ritual of giving and receiving in front of an altar. This is a chance to realize that the rakusu, which you have spent many hours sewing over the course of weeks or months, does not really belong to you. All your hard work is now in the hands of another. When it is time, the teacher will return the rakusu in the Jukai or Zaike Tokudo (lay initiation) ceremony, when you will be fully initiated into the teachings you will embody over time. I see it as a fusing of the self into a consciousness of liberation. You receive a dharma name during the Jukai ceremony, which is to receive and grow the new state of mind that was accessed in the ritual of sewing. It is a name of freedom and also one to continue the infusion of the teachings. You are not being initiated into a club or even a religion as much as beginning a life of vow. You make your vows publicly known in ceremony, witnessed by your family, community, or your many communities in gratitude for their part in your transformation, and also to enact accountability for how you vow to walk in the world. After initiation, the precepts serve as guidelines when attending future retreats and sesshins.

After fifteen years in Nichiren Buddhism and six years of Zen practice, I took another level of initiation, priest ordination, which is moving into a more expansive life in which we let go more and more of worldly affairs. There are few books that use the lens of ritual and ceremony to examine the process of ordaining as a priest in Zen, so I choose to share here from a teacher from an African tradition I met many years ago. In her book on the African Yoruba-Lukumi tradition, *Finding Soul on the Path of Orisa*, Tobe Melora Correal writes that to become a priest "means walking away from our persona, the carefully constructed false self whose main concern is image. . . . Image must be annihilated in order for transformation to take place."[2] In this same sense, the Zen ceremony of Shukke Tokudo is furthering awakening by uncluttering your life. You are especially looking to clear out the things that draw you away from the stillness and silence needed to see the true vastness of life.

Conducted in a sacred way, the Zen ritual of ordination can bring you closer to the radiance that brought us to this earth. Experiencing ordination is an important step toward being able to offer ceremony to others. As Correal writes, "It is not what we know, but how wisely, compassionately, and humbly we use our knowledge [of ritual and ceremony]."[3] If ritual is performed with an intellectual mind or if your suffering is so great, you are only reinforcing it in your prayer or meditation, then the possibility of touching God, or the source of life that brought us to this earth, will be lost. Correal continues, "Whatever the nature of the ritual, its purpose is always to pay homage to the sacred nature of all life."[4] There is no striving in entering priesthood. It is instead the ritual acknowledgment of what is already here—awakening or enlightenment.

In taking lay initiation, you commit to the teachings for the first time. In accepting priest ordination, you commit for the second time. You recommit to the vows taken in Zaike Tokudo and enter Shukke Tokudo. In 2008, upon entering priesthood, I received bowls, lineage papers, and an *okesa* (also known as a *kashaya* in Sanskrit), which is the longer robe that crosses over the left shoulder of all ordained monks and nuns in the Buddhist tradition. The robe is not separate from the teachings. We respectfully unfold the robe and place it on our bodies as the teachings. Some robes today are made of fancy material, while others sew robes from worn fabric pieces in the fashion of mendicant monks. In either case, the okesa is symbolically much more than a piece of cloth.

In ancient times, the wearing of the robe was considered to have the power to liberate us. Teachings on the okesa are found in the third chapter, "Kesa-kudoku" ("Virtue of the Kashaya"), of Dogen's *Treasury of the True Dharma Eye*. As translated by contemporary Zen teacher Shohaku Okumura, the robe, "which is the one robe like the Dharma, has been transmitted from buddha to buddha, ancestor to ancestor. The original robe is still kept at the Baolin Temple (Horinji) on Mt. Caoxi."[5] The "original robe" here refers to that of the Sixth Ancestor, Eno.[6] Emperors hosted the robe at their imperial palaces to make offerings and pay homage to the robe of dharma. It was a sacred object to be protected and maintained. It is also said that we are born with an okesa— we are born with our buddha nature. To put on an okesa is self-liberation and complete transformation because it represents awakening to our buddha nature. This is said of the okesa in the Okesa Sutra:

> The dragon with even a thread of the okesa is able to escape from the hazard of falling prey to the garuda, the king of birds. Crossing the sea carrying the okesa, by no means are you concerned about the danger of the dragon, fish, or other devils. Even a thunderbolt or an unforeseen disaster, fear is kept away from those who wear the okesa.[7]

Those who receive Denkai, dharma transmission, enter a third ceremony and for a third time commit to the vows taken in lay initiation. It is also the second ceremonial passage that involves sewing an okesa. Each time taking refuge in the Buddha, Dharma, and Sangha, you deepen your intuition, wisdom, and insight.

Dharma transmission is a private process between teacher and student. I found it to be the most shamanic of all Zen rituals and ceremonies. Although some share its details, it is not wise to do so. The secret aspect could be misunderstood by those who are not engaging in the rituals and ceremonies. To simply hear about it secondhand is to demote the process to a story and dilute its significance. I did share with my students some activities that were not secret such as the many altars that were constructed in my home, where I began the process. With permission, I was approved to invite my students to join me in the first weeks of bowing. Toward the end of my dharma transmission, however, I was sequestered in the temple, away from students and the public, to render the ritual of calligraphy, chanting, bowing, and private ceremonies. In the end, a new set of robes are offered, and the robes that have been worn up to that point are returned to the center for future use by others who may need them.

Dharma transmission is a ritual to pass on a family legacy, that family extending from the Buddha to one's own transmission. In his essay "Dharma Transmission in Theory and Practice," the scholar William M. Bodiford details how Zen dharma transmission was originally structured to accord with Confucian norms concerning family structure. Looking at the similarity between Chinese terms used to describe family roles and dharma family roles, Bodiford writes, "To be ordained is to join a dharma family that functions exactly like any other family, with the same Confucian family values and the same Confucian family expectations and obligations."[8] Although medieval Chinese Buddhism included forms of pluralism, such as different schools and monastics visiting from other Asian countries, it saw nothing like the plurality of ethnicities and cultures present in American Buddhism today. For contemporary Western Zen Buddhists, it is important to respectfully take one's place within the centuries-old "family" model of ordination and transmission, yet it can be troubling for some Western Zen students to think of ourselves as "heirs" of the teachers and teachings given our various ethnicities and ways of being. To be inclusive of many lineages of teachers, I included in my dharma transmission ceremony various altars to black women writers who transformed my life as well as to spirits of Vodou that were similar in my eyes to the ones in Zen. I also created an altar with all the shawls I was gifted during six years as head drummer and singer of a Native American Sundance ceremony.

That was my way of becoming a dharma heir as my whole self. But how do we as communities recognize a Zen practice family of mixed race and heritage? Can this recognition become a regular part of dharma transmission ceremonies? In the absolute sense, it is true that to be transmitted the dharma is to become an heir of the teachings, which do not have any ethnic, racial, or gender identity. But in the relative view, we are heirs to the teachers, starting with Buddha, who did and do exist with such identities. On my lineage papers, a long line of teachers from Asia leads up to my own teacher, an American woman with Jewish heritage. In a sense, this diversification of the Buddhist lineage family simply reflects what is happening at large in society. I once saw john a. powell, a scholar and director of the Othering & Belonging Institute in Berkeley, California, ask a roomful of people to stand if their family is of mixed race and heritage. Almost everyone in a room of about two hundred stood, including me. It was a profound moment to look into each other's faces and witness our interrelationship and belonging to each other. Yet, such recognition does not erase the difficulties of calling each other family in the midst of oppression. This is true in society and it is true with dharma transmission in Zen practice. I think it is natural for there to be a struggle to embrace the role of heir to the Buddha from ancient India and to each other. It is not so simple to follow a process of dharma transmission that is embedded in the ancient social norms of Confucian family structure and is now also saturated with the social expectations of Western culture.

When I hear folks say they want to receive dharma transmission, I sometimes want to shake my head. The rituals involved are binding. Most practitioners are not ready for what will come of them during and after the ceremony. Even if one disrobes, the rituals and ceremonies seal your bond to the teacher and the teachings, to constant ceremony, and to awakening over and over. It can be exhausting.

．˚．

After engaging in the dharma transmission ritual, I wanted to disrobe for many reasons. A prominent one was the feeling of having joined a family in which I was comfortable in ritual but uncomfortable in relationship. Also, as one of a few dharma-transmitted teachers of African descent in the country, the onslaught of attention, teaching requests from across the United States, and projections from the wider sangha caused me to pause. Zen students of color and those from other traditions had been waiting for someone like me to closely work with them one-on-one. My heart said yes, but my body could not meet all the requests. I could not be "the one."

I was told my teacher had the same response of wanting to disrobe after her dharma transmission. What were we running away from after decades of Zen practice? I can't speak for my teacher, but I can say that I thought I was caught up in something I didn't want to be. The ceremony of dharma transmission affected me in deep ways I am still unable to speak about. I wanted to be of no-rank, as they say in Zen, and go on about my business, leaving behind projections of the Zen teacher.

It wasn't until I officiated my first Jukai for my students that living a life of vow came into full view. I saw that the transmission wasn't about me. Through my tears, I saw my black students move with so much courage in a ceremony unfamiliar to them—hand-in-hand, heart-to-heart, into full liberation. Not liberation from something but liberation into being the body of nature, being the earth that they are. It was difficult to stop crying as I said these words: "Abiding according to the Ten Grave Precepts, even after realizing Buddhahood, will you continuously observe them?" The initiates responded, "Yes, I will."

During the Jukai, I performed the ancient water purification ritual, Abhisheka, with the wisdom water cup I was gifted during dharma transmission. (The cup is bestowed along with the hossu whisk, kotsu staff, bowls, and robes.) I stood at the altar and chanted, as taught to me, an ancient secret and shamanic Vajrayana Buddhist ritual verse. The chant is done over a bowl of water that is alchemically and symbolically transformed into wisdom water. I chanted with the index finger of my right hand swirling the water while holding my left hand in what's called a vajra mudra, which looks like a fist. Afterward, I touched my head with a pine twig that had a few leaves, drawing out the wisdom of the Buddha that was transmitted to me in the secret dharma transmission ceremony. I placed the twig in the water three times to make sure. I then offered the wisdom water to the entire assembly by tossing sprinkles to the bowed heads, in four directions. I took the same sprig and same wisdom water and made secret gestures over the water. With the wisdom water and the pine twig, I walked over to my students and placed Buddha's wisdom into their heads one by one.

In the water ritual, I am no longer Zenju. I am a conduit for Buddha's love and liberation. The Abhisheka ritual ends with me returning the wisdom water to the altar, chanting with the vajra mudra, and taking the wisdom of Buddha back from the water into my head.

Through this first ritual with the wisdom water, I saw the students' devotion to awakening and the joy on their faces. Witnessing them receive a dharma name as a mantra free from oppression and sensing the potential for their greater freedom, I decided to keep the robe, which is to keep the approval to lead rituals and ceremonies. I would keep the robe if only to stand at the gate and usher in those—no matter their background and no matter if they identify as Zen or Buddhist—who want to live free, filled with love, and be protected from harm in doing so.[9]

A RITUAL OF SUSTENANCE FOR RESTLESS SPIRITS

As a child born on October 31 — Halloween—I resonate with the Zen ceremony of Seijiki, which is shamanic to the core. One of the most important ceremonies of the year, it honors ancestors and the spirit world. It is. The chant used in the ceremony, *The Gate of Sweet Dew*, says it all:

> Giving rise to the awakened mind, we uncondition-
> ally offer up a bowl of pure food to all the hungry
> ghosts in every land to the farthest reaches of vast
> emptiness in the ten directions, including every atom
> throughout the entire dharma realm. We invite all
> our departed ancestors going back to ancient times,
> the spirits dwelling in mountains, rivers, and earth,

as well as rough demonic spirits from the untamed wilderness, to come and gather here. Now, with deep sympathy we offer food to all of you, sincerely hoping that you will each accept this food and turn it over, making offerings to buddhas, sages, and all sentient beings throughout the vast emptiness of the universe, so that you and all the many sentient beings will be satisfied. Moreover, we sincerely wish that your bodies be conveyed by these mantras and food so that you may depart from suffering, be liberated, find birth in heaven, and receive joy. In accordance with your intentions, may you travel freely through the pure lands in the ten directions and arouse awakened mind practicing the awakened way and in the future become a buddha without regressing. We entreat those who have previously attained the way since ancient times to vow to realize liberation with all other beings together. Day and night, constantly protect us so that our vows will be fulfilled. We offer food to beings throughout the dharma realm, so that every being will equally receive this fortunate offering. Whatever virtue and merit this produces, we completely transfer and dedicate to the unsurpassed awakening with total clarity and wisdom of the whole dharma realm of true reality, that all may speedily attain buddhahood without incurring any other destinies. May all sentient beings of the dharma realm take advantage of this teaching to quickly attain buddhahood.[10]

In the Seijiki ceremony, we offer the sustenance of ritual and ceremony to reach those restless spirits who need the food medicine from it—so they too can live in abiding awareness and awakening. Much like in African ceremonies, an elaborate altar with food and flowers is constructed. Participants dress in costume or mask themselves so that the spirits are unaware of who is in the room. Such masquerading is also done in the ancient rituals for the Mexican Day of the Dead and in Haiti's and Louisiana's Fete Guede, or the Vodou Festival of the Dead, when participants converge onto the cemeteries to ritually honor ancestors. If the dead are not satisfied, there is continued disruption and suffering in our world. In other words, no matter how much we practice, these entities can wreak havoc. And yet, these enraged spirits can offer protection from danger, helping us to fulfill our vows.

Some practitioners, uncomfortable with the idea of ghosts, spirits, or devils, find it difficult to participate in Seijiki. Although I love this ceremony because it is on my birthday, I also have caution about participating because all who participate are not aware of the seriousness of the ritual. I refrain from masking for fear that my true nature as a woman of spirit, who divines the ancestors for others, would emerge and no one would know what to do with me. So, I enjoy on the surface where fun is abundant and joy is seen in the eyes of most. During the liberation of hungry ghosts, we are taking on suffering and transforming it into buddhahood. Our practice must be strong enough to withstand the calling in of ghosts and devils.

Many may laugh at this point. But I ask, how are you engaging the mind and body in Zen practice? Is it not through the rituals and ceremonies, which are interrelated to each other and zazen? You would have to step away altogether to not be a part of Seijiki, and perhaps some have done exactly that. But to pick and choose what you participate in is to reduce Zen practice to a menu of assorted flavors, which is not the complete lived experience of ritual and ceremony.

We don't know who or what we are, why we are here, and where we are going. Zen rituals and ceremonies can act as a mirror in the dark unknown of the present and in the light of the ancient past. Is there a willingness to look in the mirror and see a reflection of ourselves without any notions of Zen or Zen practice? Can we go through the flesh of the tradition as presented and consider the bones? The teachings received in talks and books are a reflection of the truth but not the truth itself. To engage the body and mind in ritual and ceremony will reveal the soul and spirit of your own life.

Offering Gratitude

We line up for the jundo. Starting from the back, the last person steps out, bends at the waist, palms joined, and slowly walks past the person next to them without facing them. Just a deep silent bow. I follow the first person, bending at the waist, palms joined walking in reverence. Others are waiting, heads bowed. When I come to those who have led the ceremonies and rituals, I stop, face them, and bow. I resume walking, bending at the waist, palms joined. Others are following behind like a river of people streaming through to say thank you. Thank you for the food, the bed, the seat in which to awaken through the challenges of life. Thank you for your patience. Thank you for showing me to myself. Thank you. Thank you. Thank you.

For all the rituals and ceremonies, there must be gratitude. Robin Wall Kimmerer, an ethnobotanist, the author of *Braiding Sweetgrass*, and a member of the Potawatomi Nation, writes in an essay for *Emergence Magazine*, "Gratitude is so much more than a polite thank you. It is the thread that connects us in a deep relationship, simultaneously physical and spiritual, as our bodies are fed and spirits nourished by the sense of belonging, which is the most vital of foods. Gratitude creates a sense of abundance, the knowing that you have what you need. In that climate of sufficiency, our hunger for more abates and we take only what we need, in respect for the generosity of the giver."[1]

In her essay "What the Buddha Taught About Gratitude," the Zen practitioner and writer Barbara O'Brien writes, "Gratitude is to be cultivated as a habit or attitude of mind not dependent on conditions. In the quote below, we see that the Buddha taught that gratitude is necessary for integrity. What does that mean?

> The Blessed One said, "Now what is the level of a person of no integrity? A person of no integrity is ungrateful and unthankful. This ingratitude, this lack of thankfulness, is advocated by rude people. It is entirely on the level of people of no integrity. A person of integrity is grateful and thankful. This gratitude, this thankfulness, is advocated by civil people. It is entirely on the level of people of integrity."[2]

Even the difficulties we are grateful for because they bring an experience of compassion. O'Brien quotes the Zen teacher Zoketsu Norman Fischer's interpretation of the meaning of lack of gratitude: "We take our life, we take life, we take existence, for granted. We take it as a given, and then we complain that it isn't working out as we wanted it to. But why should we be here in the first place? Why should we exist at all?"[3]

It is difficult to say thank you in the midst of the struggle. Yet I have experienced gratitude as inclusive of hardships. If there is a long enough pause, many of us experience profound insight that we can use for the rest of our lives. And in that, we are more grateful for life, whether it is up or down.

After gratitude, there is reciprocity, says Robin Wall Kimmerer.[4] I have experienced this myself. After every sun dance ceremony, there is a thank you ceremony in which everyone gives back by gifting things that we may have held onto for years. The meaning changes when we see those things as gifts. We are grateful for prayers, transformation, food, songs, tears, and the land. In many Buddhist centers—though not so much in Zen centers—students give gifts to the teachers in the form of *dana* (the Sanskrit for "generosity"). This custom was originally giving alms, and in Western sanghas, it is giving money as a practice of generosity. Once I had a juban and kimono made for my teacher because I had seen holes in her old ones. Some give calligraphy, tea, incense, or books to fellow sojourners or to teachers after a week-long ritual of zazen. It is crucial that we close our rituals and ceremonies with acts of gratitude. These acts can be just the words "thank you." Even a silent bow, done wholeheartedly and with a sense of connection, is a gift.

I bow to all that crosses my path.

Afterword

In the book *The Wisdom of the Shamans*, Don Jose Ruiz
writes that in the Toltec tradition of South-Central Mexico,
a shaman is called a *nagual*. But the word also has a second
meaning: "the life force energy and divinity within all
beings."[1] A nagual is a shaman who is awakened to this.
Ruiz writes that we all have the same life force energy as
a shaman, but many have not realized this. He goes on to
say that spiritual traditions that are shamanic have at least
these three qualities: respect for nature, respect for all life,
and respect for their ancestors. And he says the wisdom of
the ancient masters, which is the wisdom of love and life,
is available to all humankind.[2] Although he holds that this
is only the tip of shamanism, I argue that those elements
already place Zen squarely in the shamanic realm.

The dream I had of the Black Angel oracle was a manifes-
tation of the life force energy that emerged from vigorously
chanting a Buddhist mantra. The dream was a truth inside
myself, and it manifested in a quest to discover the wisdom
of love and life. I was my own shaman. No one teacher in
Zen or in any other tradition could bring me to this real-

ization. However, the teachers, diviners, and chiefs I have followed in ceremony did, with great generosity, provide a place to safely journey inward toward that dream, toward a life I did not know existed. They provided the territory by which I could dance into and experience divinity in all of life, including Zen. I stayed to see more and more.

Ruiz says we are all messengers of truth and love. Somehow, we know this deep in our hearts. I offer gratitude to those who hold the space for what is in our hearts, which is to hold the divine, the sacred, the soul, and the spirit.

No doubt there are some who are skeptical of the unearthing I have done here, or maybe suspicious of the deeper look I am requesting of contemporary Zen practitioners. Some have looked me in the face and asked, "Why?" And I have seen the question, "Just what are you doing?" written on people's faces. I have finally written down my response the best I could. My calling was not to wear robes, to be an accepted black darling in a predominantly white Zen environment, or to further the inherent tokenism I have experienced. I saw the sacredness even though others, inside and outside the monastery, didn't see such. Granted, there are many things that can distract anyone from seeing the bones of Zen that were buried back in India, China, and Japan. Perhaps those who were confused simply experienced my search for the bones as another distraction. I could only smile when I saw confusion on their faces. I had come with my medicine in hand, to lay it down on the altar of Zen and see what shape it would take. To see what it would look like after the alchemical process of transformation was complete. A shaman tests their medicine in many places with many people.

I found in me a person speaking who once could not speak her truth. I found this person who cared about others' lives, but who once didn't see anyone because she thought they didn't see her. This is all to say I came to know myself because I came to know life and how to live on this star called Earth. I could have come to these discoveries on any path of spirit. By path of spirit, I mean any way that is felt as a gateway to freedom from the things that bind me. My blackness does not bind me. Only when blackness does not evolve from its beginnings am I trapped by it. Even if there were no systems of oppression, there would be something else in life I would have to contend with. There would be other hard grounds to till through and add new soil and water. I can be of service to the earth and to others as earth, whether they think of themselves as students or not. My service can take the form of ritual and ceremony, Zen or not. For me, there is no substance in being a Zen teacher if not to lead ritual and ceremony—indoors or outdoors.

I am constantly asked to give dharma talks, as that has become the way. But talks, in the way they are usually structured, cannot engage the mind and body in the way ritual and ceremony can. I seek to offer talks that are fluid—not time- or topic-driven, without a sense of gaining knowledge. A seeing and listening experience, but not with the eyes or ears. To remain in zazen during a dharma talk is to remain in ritual, and that is how I was taught. Through engagement with your own soul and spirit, you come to your own words. And with guidance from one soul to another, your words come from the spirit of your being and not from your suffering or from another's view. When I was twenty, one modern-day sage told me, "One day, you will stop speaking of your suffering. Then, you will know God." She didn't say, "Your suffering will end." My story of suffering continued to pour from my gut for many more years after that encounter with the sage. My past, prior to entering Zen life, was filled with various transgressions against myself and others. After years of practice, I spoke less on my own suffering and more on the suffering of all human beings.

When I speak of how I've suffered, it is only to reveal my human frailty, speak from a place of humility, and model that, despite suffering, we can eventually come to live upright in integrity. I feel myself more in the image of God or as an expression of the infinite. I had to learn this. Not from a book or a teacher, but from walking upon the embers of great fires, step by step. Sometimes pain, sometimes bliss.

.°.

Zen isn't for everyone. It's a rare person who is ready to go down in the belly of the whale, to be chewed up and spit out. Meditation in general, when approached with sincere spiritual intention, is a tough shamanic experience. It takes whatever you have and turns it into something else; one can feel boiled into another form of oneself. Most of us are not able to handle the alchemical changes that can occur. Trauma can arise and run rapidly through the body, and meditating on the trauma is dangerous territory. The trauma can be so present that one cannot hear or understand the teachers, as one fears dying in the depth of a deep dive. And yet, we are to bring our entire being to the altar. The entire being, traumatized or not, is available for peace and awakening. The question is, are you willing to experience love? Not a manufactured love that comes from your mind and is given and taken at will. It is a love that comes from a source unknown. A strong practice without experiencing buddha love is nothing.

In the San Francisco Bay, there is a place called Goat Rock Beach where the Russian River meets the Pacific Ocean. On their way to each other, it appears as though it is a river meeting the ocean. But it is simply water meeting water. When we are in ritual or ceremony, we are water meeting water. We bring our fire, earth, and breath; we bring our human selves. Whether I succeed or not, by whatever measure, at anything in the eyes of those outside looking in, I am grateful for the journey. We are only passing through to learn, to grow, to love, and then we return home.

Chants Created by
Zenju Earthlyn Manuel

FOR ALL BEINGS

influenced by the Metta Sutra, or Loving-Kindness Sutra

May all beings be cared for and loved,
Be listened to, understood, and acknowledged,
     despite different views,
Be accepted for who they are in this moment,
Be afforded patience,
Be allowed to live without fear of having their lives
     taken away or their bodies violated.
May all beings,
Be well in its broadest sense,
Be fed,
Be clothed,
Be treated as if their life is precious,
Be held in the eyes of each other as family.
May all beings,
Be appreciated,
Feel welcomed anywhere on the planet,
Be freed from acts of hatred and desperation
     including war, poverty, slavery, and street crimes,

Live on the planet, housed, and protected from harm,
Be given what is needed to live fully, without scarcity,
Enjoy life, living without fear of one another,
Be able to speak freely in a voice and mind of
    undeniable love.
May all beings,
receive and share the gifts of life,
Be given time to rest, be still, and experience silence.
May all beings,
Be awake.

HEARTS OF NIRVANA

Based on the Yogacara by Vasubandhu

May the great way of easing suffering be passed on for
    generations,
beginning with planting the seeds of enlightenment,
that lead to hearts of enlightenment,
that lead to fields of wisdom and compassion,
that lead to the pathway of liberation.
May the seeds of suffering be uprooted for the sake of
    all beings,
and may the seeds of infinite joy be spread throughout
    the world,
ending the roots of harm, hatred, and
    misunderstanding,
ending the roots of hostility, hypocrisy, envy, and
    selfishness,
ending the roots of supremacy and false pride of any
    kind.

May the afflictions within our stories of suffering be
    revealed,
knowing that all who suffer, suffer the same
    afflictions,
Knowing that all life is transforming, ever-flowing,
every moment is a chance to plant new seeds,
new seeds that create new and selfless acts of love,
new seeds that endure throughout time,
new seeds that represent our inherent
    interrelationship,
which represents the whole cosmos.
May the seeds of enlightenment come forth from
    within,
illuminating hearts of enchantment,
hearts of clarity and complete perception,
hearts of awareness of all bodies and minds,
hearts of non-judgment.
There is nirvana in all beings and in all things,
all consciousnesses are within all other consciousness,
all seeds exist before they exist and need only be
    planted to be born,
all beings exist before they exist and need only be
    planted to be born.
When there is no coming or no going amid
    conditions,
No-being or non-being amid conditions,
there is nirvana.

I Can Breathe

May I come back to this body,
May I come back to this breath,
May I come to know this body as the earth itself.
May I breathe myself back home,
And once again be introduced to this great life.

May the great light of this Earth surround me,
May I be released from past harm and imposed hatred.
May I come to recognize my existence in the true
    nature of life.
May I come back to this breath,
to this body, as the sacred place in which I remain
    awake
and connected to the fragrance and taste of liberation.

May I remain visible on the path of spirit,
and be seen and heard,
May love given be returned tenfold,
May awakening be known in this body,
at this time.

And when I can't breathe,
May I breathe in the next moment,
May I say, I can breathe.

Eric Garner, a black man, father of six, was choked to death by Staten Island, New York, police in July 2014. A film shot from a smartphone recorded Garner's words, "I can't breathe."

Guidelines for Entering, Abiding, and Departing Long Meditation Retreats and Sesshins

Adjustments can be made if the retreat is online, including online posture and appropriate environment around the computer, dress, and state of mind.

Many ask, "How do I enter into a silent meditation ritual/retreat and then re-engage the world upon departure?" Buddhist retreats are not of the "spa" nature but more of a shamanic ritual with deep work within and without. Due to the shamanic effects of meditation, I have shared these guidelines for entering, participating, and departing rituals at home or at retreat centers. The silence will expand the territory of your life and may align you with your breath and perhaps allow life to unfold without tampering with it for a day, week, month, or however long your journey of engaging your mind and body. Eventually, retreats will be seamless—you come and you go. Also retreats will become seamless between your life and the scheduled retreats—just another day. But here are a few suggestions you can adjust to your life:

Entering Rituals

- A week to two weeks prior to the time of your retreat, go to bed early, rise early, sit, eat less (eat mostly green vegetables and brown or forbidden rice, and consume less sugar, salt, etc.)
- Drink calming teas such as tulsi (holy basil).
- Reduce or eliminate alcoholic and caffeinated drinks. Discuss the use of cannabis or other medications with your practice leader as to whether or not it will interfere with your sit. Take your usual medications and do not expect to be cured through meditation.
- Read less; view less TV (news, movies, etc.); lessen phone, email, and social media use; and reduce work and contact with others. Less, less, less. . . .
- Rest, rest, and more rest. Do not go to retreat to rest. Catch up on your sleep so that you are *awake* for the ceremony. Come energized and do not look for the retreat to energize you.
- Walk more than usual to move angst through the body.
- Bathe more often.
- Refrain from any serious conversations or dialogues that need processing but cannot be completed before your retreat.
- Let your friends and family know you are gifting yourself with silence and express gratitude for how they have supported you thus far in your journey of life. You want them to feel you are taking them with you in your heart and that it is for them as well, the family, community, and the world at large.
- If you are driving to the retreat or have to drive on the days of your silence, no music, no news, and no conversation if possible.

- Put down all books you are reading (including spiritual books) and all writing (including journaling).
- Let go of projects you are working on at least three days in advance.
- Arrange to have a day off before and a day off after the retreat if possible.
- Arrange for someone you really trust to sit with children, elders, ill family members, and/or pets or take care of plants, bills, and anything that needs taking care of in your absence.
- Do not bring a lot of belongings from home, especially things that might remind you to "do something." Keep everything to bare necessities. Simple. Just a cell phone for emergency calls only. Leave the iPad and computer if you can.

Abiding in Rituals

- When your retreat starts, take in *each moment* as the retreat and not see yourself as sitting for a *whole* day, week, month, or however long your retreat is. Take in each moment of the retreat as it reveals the true seamlessness of life. No matter what relative time has been set, it is an infinite experience.
- See the retreat as an extension of the life you are living right now, as a continuum, no different, just one day breathing and seeing, walking, eating . . . then another day, doing the same. Seeing the mundane life as it is. Without toys. Possibly the monotony will disappear and be replaced with insight and wisdom.
- Reduce your portions of food; much is not needed while

sitting still. Avoid fasting unless your retreat calls for such and the leader has recommended it.

- Congratulate yourself for taking time out of your life to commit to an act of love for yourself. Everyone around will receive such love.
- Carry an inner smile. Laugh at the mind. Let thoughts arise without stopping to engage them.
- Allow the schedule to be that which you fall back into freedom, away from your daily life. You do not have to do anything but let your body settle back into the time you are giving it to pause.
- Let the politics of life go for this time. We who believe in freedom *can* rest and justice *will be done* with a well and rested body and mind.
- Enjoy being a sleuth in the mystery of your life.
- While retreating, you have an opportunity to cease harming, worry, shift habits, and behavior. You can simply witness your life as you move through each moment.
- Express your concerns or any abuses in a spiritual discussion with a spiritual companion or teacher. If no one is available, write your concerns down until you can speak with someone who can provide appropriate guidance. Avoid gossip or talking behind someone's back.
- Let the retreat leaders know if you are struggling and need help. Let them know of any harm that is coming toward you based on race, sexuality, or gender of any kind. Don't leave without notifying them. Don't expect resolution. Expect that everyone is coming with an edge or with some kind of suffering, including the teachers.
- Competing with other retreatants will rob you of a beautiful respite.

- Look out into the open land, sky, or ocean and see it as your life—vast, open, empty of clutter (an image you can carry inside you).
- Cry if you must. Cry if you can.
- Let go and breathe.

DEPARTING RITUALS

- Congratulate yourself again.
- Let go of insights that appeared during your retreat. They will return when you need them.
- Keep experience to yourself for a while. Let the cooking of your life settle. Say to your friends, "I gave myself a wonderful gift and I am still being with it."
- Let your loved ones know you care about what happened while you were away, but you would like to talk about it the next day if it's not an emergency.
- Nourish yourself like you would a newborn.
- Try not to spend time judging your experience—good or bad, successful or not.
- Continue to sit and settle your thinking on the breath. Build on the experience.
- Listen to everything. Listen to the sounds around you. Listen to those who are speaking. Listen longer than usual. Listen.
- Engage in activities that are in alignment with an experience of peace. Take nature walks. Bathe. Get a massage.
- Avoid parties or large gatherings for some time.
- Avoid long conversations.
- Avoid returning to work on the day the retreat ends and the day after if possible.

- Once you return to work, set the timer on your cell phone (or computer) to sound every thirty minutes to remind you of the breath and experience of the retreat.
- Set three times of the day you will answer emails and return calls instead of every time you receive a message.
- Let your coworkers know you are having a slow day (no need to say the reason unless you are compelled to).
- Live the teachings for some time and wait a while to speak to others about what you have learned. Consider how much you would share and for what reasons.
- Cherish every moment as you did in the silence—the difficult and the not so difficult.

Notes

RATTLING THE BONES

1. Robert Scharf, "Ritual," in *Critical Terms for the Study of Buddhism*, ed. Donald S. Lopez (Chicago: University of Chicago Press, 2005), 248–249.
2. Sam van Schaik, *Tibetan Zen: Discovering a Lost Tradition* (Boulder: Snow Lion, 2015).
3. T. Griffith Foulk, "Denial of Ritual in the Zen Buddhist Tradition," *Journal of Ritual Studies* 27, no. 1 (2013): 47–58; https://www.jstor.org/stable/44368864.
4. Foulk, "Denial of Ritual," 51.
5. Steven Heine and Dale S. Wright, eds., *Zen Ritual: Studies of Zen Theory and Practice* (Oxford: Oxford University Press, 2008), 4.
6. *Online Etymological Dictionary*, s.v. "shaman," https://www.etymonline.com/word/shaman#etymonline_v_23334.
7. Sam van Schaik, *Buddhist Magic: Divination, Healing, and Enchantment through the Ages* (Boulder: Shambhala, 2020), 2, 4.
8. Foulk, "Denial of Ritual," 47.

Preparing the Sanctuary for Ritual

1. Philip B. Yampolsky, trans., *The Zen Master Hakuin: Selected Writings* (New York: Columbia University Press, 1971), 58.
2. Shitou, "Song of the Grass-Roof Hermitage," trans. Taigen Dan Leighton and Kazuaki Tanahashi in *Inside the Grass Hut: Living Shitou's Classic Zen Poem*, ed. Ben Connelly (Somerville, MA: Wisdom, 2014), 11.

Making Offerings to the Ancestors

1. Bryan Cuevas, The *All-Pervading Melodious Drumbeat: The Life of Ra Lotsawa* (New York: Penguin, 2015), xx. See also van Schaik, *Buddhist Magic*, 3.
2. Bradley S. Clough, "The Higher Knowledges in the Pali Nikayas and Vinaya," *Journal of the International Association of Buddhist Studies* 33, no. 1–2, (2011), 409.
3. Clough, "Higher Knowledges," 410.
4. Paula K. R. Arai, "Women and Dogen: Rituals Actualizing Empowerment and Healing," in *Zen Ritual: Studies of Zen Buddhist Theory in Practice*, ed. Steven Heine and Dale S. Wright (Oxford: Oxford University Press, 2008), 185.

Prolonged Rituals of Seeing and Listening

1. Shunryu Suzuki, *Zen Mind, Beginner's Mind* (New York: Weatherhill, 1970), 5.
2. Dainin Katagiri, *Returning to Silence* (Boulder: Shambhala, 1988), 39.

3. Stephen Addiss, *The Art of Zen* (New York: Henry N. Abrams, 1989), 206, footnote 1.

4. Charlotte Eubanks, "Performing Mind, Writing Meditation: Dogen's *Fukanzazengi* as Zen Calligraphy," *Ars Orientalis*, https://doi.org/10.3998/ars.13441566.0046.007.

5. Isa Gucciardi, "The Journey: Buddhism and Shamanism at the Crossroads," *Sacred Stream*, https://www.sacredstream.org/the-journey-buddhism-and-shamanism-at-the-crossroads/, accessed April 27, 2021.

6. Philip Kapleau, *The Three Pillars of Zen: Teaching, Practice, and Enlightenment* (New York: Anchor, 2000), 7.

7. Meido Moore, *Hidden Zen: Practices for Sudden Awakening and Embodied Realization* (Boulder: Shambhala, 2020), 9–10.

8. Daisetz Teitaro Suzuki, *Introduction to Zen Buddhism* (New York: Grove Press, 1964), 96.

9. Moore, *Hidden Zen*, 12, emphasis in original.

10. Philip Kapleau, *The Three Pillars of Zen: Teaching, Practice, and Enlightenment* (New York: Anchor Books, 1980), 49–53.

11. Kapleau, *Three Pillars of Zen*, 50.

12. Taigen Dan Leighton, *Zen Questions: Zazen, Dogen, and the Spirit of Creative Inquiry* (Somerville, MA: Wisdom, 2011), 25.

13. See Taigen Dan Leighton, "Zazen as an Enactment Ritual," in *Zen Ritual: Studies of Zen Buddhist Theory in Practice*, ed. Steven Heine and Dale S. Wright (Oxford: Oxford University Press, 2008), 167.

14. See for instance, Taigen Dan Leighton, "Zazen as an Enactment Ritual," Ancient Dragon Zen Gate (March 2, 2019), https://www.ancientdragon.org/za-zen-as-enactment-ritual/, accessed May 10, 2021. For a deep look at the role of esoteric practice in medieval Japanese Buddhism, see Jacqueline I. Stone, *Original Enlightenment and the Transformation of Medieval Japanese Buddhism* (Honolulu: University of Hawaii Press, 1999).

15. "Fukanzazengi of Eihei Dogen," https://www.sfzc.org/files/daily_sutras_Fukanzazengi, 21–22.

CHANTING SPELLS

1. Kazuaki Tanahashi, *Zen Chants: Thirty-Five Essential Texts with Commentary* (Boulder: Shambhala, 2015), 11.

2. Stephen Slottow, *The Americanization of Zen Chanting* (Hillsdale, NY: Pendragon Press, 2019), 3, 1.

3. Tanahashi, *Zen Chants*, 7–8.

4. James Nestor, *Breath: The New Science of a Lost Art* (New York: Riverhead, 2020), ix.

5. Tanahashi, *Zen Chants*, 11–12.

6. Daining Katagiri, *Returning to Silence: Zen Practice in Daily Life* (Boulder: Shambhala, 1988), 67, 71–72

7. Van Schaik, *Buddhist Magic*, 69–70, 74.

8. Richard D. McBride, "Wish-Fulfilling Spells and Talismans, Efficacious Resonance, and Trilingual Spell Books: The *Mahapratisara-dharaṇi* in Choson Buddhism," *Pacific World*, no. 20 (2018): 57.

9. McBride, "Wish-Fulfilling Spells and Talismans," 57.

10. "Dharaṇi Sutras," in *Brill's Encyclopedia of Buddhism*,

ed. J. Silk, O. von Hinyber, and V. Eltschinger (Leiden: Brill, 2015), 1:134.

11. Tanahashi, *Zen Chants*, 138.

12. Kazuaki Tanahashi and Joan Halifax, trans., *The Mystical Blue-Necked One Avalokiteshvara or the Great Compassionate Heart Dharani* (unpublished, 2003). Used by permission.

Rituals of Celebration and Initiation

1. Dale S. Wright, "Introduction: Rethinking Ritual Practice in Zen Buddhism," in *Zen Ritual: Studies of Zen Buddhist Theory in Practice*, ed. Wright and Heine (Oxford: Oxford University Press, 2008), 10–11.

2. Tobe Melora Correal, *Finding Soul on the Path of Orisa: A West African Spiritual Tradition* (Berkeley, CA: Crossing Press, 2003), 168.

3. Correal, *Finding Soul*, 46.

4. Correal, *Finding Soul*, 79.

5. Shohaku Okumura, *Kesa-Kudoku (Virtue of Kashaya)*, unpublished booklet, 1.

6. Rev. Kenshu Sugawara, *Kesa Kudoku: Virtue of the Kashaya*, https://www.yumpu.com/en/document/read/38647813/kesa-kudoku-virtue-of-the-kashaya-sotozen-net, accessed May 12, 2021.

7. Quoted from study materials used at San Francisco Zen Center during the sewing of an okesa.

8. William M. Bodiford, "Dharma Transmission in Theory and Practice," in *Zen Ritual: Studies of Zen Buddhist Theory in Practice*, ed. Steven Heine and Dale

S. Wright (Oxford: Oxford University Press, 2008), 267–268.

9. This section was shared from an essay I authored for *Buddhadharma* magazine. Zenju Earthlyn Manuel, "Living My Vow," February 24, 2021, *Buddhadharma*, www.lionsroar.com/living-my-vow.

10. From the *San Francisco Zen Center Chant Book.*

OFFERING GRATITUDE

1. Robin Wall Kimmerer, "The Serviceberry: An Economy of Abundance," *Emergence Magazine*, Dec. 10, 2020, www.emergencemagazine.org/essay/the-serviceberry/, accessed May 12, 2021.

2. Barbara O'Brien, "What the Buddha Taught about Gratitude," *Learn Religions*, February 18, 2019, www.learnreligions.com/being-grateful-449576, accessed May 12, 2021. The excerpt within the quote is from the Katannu Sutta (AN 2.31–32), translated from the Pali by Thanissaro Bhikkhu, available at https://www.accesstoinsight.org/tipitaka/an/an02/an02.031.than.html.

3. O'Brien, "What the Buddha Taught about Gratitude."

4. Kimmerer, "The Serviceberry."

AFTERWORD

1. Don Jose Ruiz, *The Wisdom of the Shamans: What the Ancient Masters Can Teach Us about Love and Life* (San Antonio, TX: Hierophant, 2019), xvii.

2. Ruiz, *The Wisdom of the Shamans*, xii, xvi.

Resources

Arai, Paula. *Bringing Zen Home: The Healing Heart of Japanese Women's Rituals* (Honolulu: University of Hawaii, 2011).

Bodiford, William M. "Dharma Transmission in Theory and Practice," in *Zen Ritual*, ed. Stephen Heine and Dale S. Wright (New York: Oxford University, 2007).

Connelly, Ben. *Inside the Grass Hut: Living Shitou's Classic Zen Poem* (Somerville, MA: Wisdom, 2014).

Correal, Tobe Melora. *Finding Soul on the Path of the Orisa: A West African Spiritual Tradition* (New York: Crossing, 2003).

Griffith Foulk, T. "The Denial of Zen Ritual," essay emailed to author.

Heine, Stephen, and Dale S. Wright. *Zen Rituals: Studies of Zen Buddhist Theory in Practice* (New York: Oxford University, 2007).

Kapleau, Philip. *The Three Pillars of Zen: Teaching, Practice and Enlightenment* (New York: Anchor, 1989).

Katagiri, Dainin. *Returning to Silence: Zen Practice in Daily Life* (Boston: Shambhala, 1988).

Leighton, Taigen Dan. "Zazen as an Enactment Ritual" in

Zen Ritual, ed. Stephen Heine and Dale S. Wright (New York: Oxford University, 2007).

Manuel, Zenju Earthlyn. *Black Angel Cards: 36 Oracle Cards and Messages for Divining Your Life* (out of print).

McBride, Richard D. *Wish-Fulfilling Spells and Talismans, Efficacious Resonance, and Trilingual Spell Books: The Mahapratisara-dharani in Choson Buddhism* (Brigham Young University, Hawaii, 2018).

Moore, Meido. *Hidden Zen: Practices for Sudden Awakening and Embodied Realization* (Boulder: Shambhala, 2020).

Nestor, James. *Breath: The New Science of a Lost Art* (New York: Riverhead Books, 2020).

O'Brien, Barbara. "Gratitude," *Learn Religions*, February 18, 2019, https://www.learnreligions.com/being-grateful-449576).

Okumura, Shohaku. *True Dharma Eye Treasury, Kesa-kudoku* (Virtue of Kashaya).

Ruiz, Don Jose. *The Wisdom of the Shamans: What the Ancient Masters Can Teach Us about Love and Life* (San Antonio, TX: Hierophant, 2018).

San Francisco Zen Center. "Chants: Gate of Sweet Dew, Dai Hi Shin Dharani, and Atonement Chant," http://www.sfzc.org.

Scharf, Robert. "Ritual" in *Critical Terms for the Study of Buddhism*, ed. Donald S. Lopez, Jr., (Chicago: University of Chicago Press, 2009).

———. "Sanbokyodan, Zen and the Way of New Religion" *Japanese Journal of Religion* no. 22, (1995), 417–58.

Slottow, Stephen P. *The Americanization of Zen Chanting* (Hillsdale, NY: Pendragon, 2018).

Tanahashi, Kaz. *Zen Chanting: Thirty-Five Essential Texts and Commentary* (Boston: Shambhala, 2015).

Wall Kimmerer, Robin. "The Serviceberry: An Economy of Abundance" *Emergence Magazine*, December 10, 2020, https://emergencemagazine.org/essay/the-serviceberry/.

van Schaik, Sam. *Buddhist Magic: Divination, Healing, and Enchantment through the Ages* (Boulder: Shambhala, 2020).

———. *Tibetan Zen: Discovering a Lost Tradition* (Boston: Snow Lion, 2015).

Wright, Dale S. "Rethinking Ritual Practice in Zen Buddhism" in *Zen Ritual*, ed. Stephen Heine and Dale S. Wright (New York: Oxford University, 2007).

About the Author

Zenju Earthlyn Manuel, PhD, poet, drum medicine woman, and ordained Zen priest, was born to parents who migrated from rural Louisiana. She was raised in the Church of Christ. Later, she followed the Nichiren Buddhist tradition/Soka Gakkai for fifteen years, eventually leading her to the path of Soto Zen. She is the dharma heir of Buddha and the late Zenkei Blanche Hartman in the Shunryu Suzuki Roshi lineage through the San Francisco Zen Center (SFZC). Her practice is influenced by Native American and African indigenous traditions including ritual, ceremony, and divination. Zenju Osho is the author of *The Deepest Peace: Contemplations from A Season of Stillness; Sanctuary: A Meditation on Home, Homelessness, and Belonging; The Way of Tenderness: Awakening through Race, Sexuality, and Gender; Tell Me Something about Buddhism*, among others. A California native, she lives in New Mexico.